Why Live That Way . . . When You Don't Have To?

Breaking Strongholds

Lee Shipp

Why Live This Way...When You Don't Have To?
by Lee Shipp

Printed in the United States of America

ISBN 978-1-60266-391-6

Unless otherwise indicated, Bible quotations are taken from he King James Version of the Bible. By Parsons Technology, Inc. Cedar Rapids, Iowa.

www.xulonpress.com

TABLE OF CONTENTS:

INTRODUCTION

B eing a pastor for more than twenty years has allowed me to see that many believers live a life they do not have to live. I am grieved as I watch so many confess a life they never experience. My heart yearns for believers to know the joyful liberty that our Lord suffered so fully to give. It is sad to see believers struggling with vices and emotional bondages when Jesus has provided a complete salvation.

I also have witnessed the awesome power of the blood of Jesus to liberate any trusting heart. From the ruins of sin and the depth of despair, I have seen Jesus powerfully bring numerous lives out of their pits!

My desire in writing this book is to answer the questions "What has to happen for the believer to enjoy the peace and victory of Jesus Christ?" "Do things have to change for me to be happy?" "Will my contentment come when people in my life begin to behave the way I want?" If that is the requirement of happiness and joy in the Lord, then nobody is going to be joyful. Thank God the joy He offers is much more durable and real.

Many in the ministry would be surprised at the number of strongholds Satan has been able to establish over the years. Is there hope for your ministry? Do you feel like giving up, thinking that you cannot work and give and serve any harder than you are and yet you cannot seem to break through? There is an awesome comfort that Jesus wants to give you. This book will encourage you and help you gain the peace that Jesus has promised. The battles are real, but so is the victory!

True spiritual warfare is not simply to get Satan out of the congregation or to control the circumstances and people that are around me. The end of all spiritual warfare is to make sure that nothing has a hold on my life except Jesus Christ. If Jesus is mine and I am His, if God be for me, then who can be against me? That is spiritual victory! That is a life free of strongholds!

You may have strongholds if:

•You are a person given to constant worry and fretting.

•You cannot get over criticism that has been brought against your life.

•You cannot bear to face certain individuals in your family, at work, or in your community.

•You have an extreme load of guilt because someone rejected you. To this day you are seeking his or her approval. You are so tired of living for his or her acceptance, but you cannot stop!

•You cannot seem to walk in the fullness of God's Spirit but frequently tend to your emotions, feelings, and suspicions.

•You cannot seem to get over the pain that has occurred in your life—the pain of rejection, the pain of abuse, the pain of betrayal.

•You cannot hope. All you can think about is quitting. You consider yourself a failure.

•You cannot bring others into the victory of Christ. Does it seem that your life is surrounded by suffering people struggling with sin who never seem to get better?

It is not time that heals; it is truth! Jesus said that you shall know the truth, and the truth shall set you free. We tend to think that rest and peace will come to us when all our circumstances are to our liking. Though this would be wonderful, it is not realistic. I rejoice in the reality of Jesus Christ to truly bring into any trusting heart all that His gospel proclaims. There is victory in Jesus, but so many seem to fight the wrong enemy . . . beating the air, as Paul put it.

There are mighty answers to destroy these strongholds that Satan has worked so hard to build. And these answers are immediate!

Everywhere you look, things may seem hopeless. It may have taken Satan years to build these things around your life. But Jesus can demolish them in a moment! Freedom is waiting for you to call!

In this book, I want to clearly reveal the victory that can take place within your life, thus bringing you into a realm of absolute rest and liberty! This is not a wishful thinking book; it is proven true in innumerable lives that I have seen transformed by the power of God. This book is grounded firmly upon the Scriptures and seeks no higher honor than to see Jesus glorified in your life and your joy exploding in the efficacy of Jesus' redemption.

Lee Shipp

DEDICATION

To all of the transformed lives who placed their faith in Jesus and proved that His gospel is as powerful today as it was 2,000 years ago!

BREAKING THE STRONGHOLD
OF THE ENEMY WITHIN

CHAPTER 1

Now I Paul myself beseech you by the meekness and gentleness of Christ, who in presence am base among you, but being absent am bold toward you: But I beseech you, that I may not be bold when I am present with that confidence, wherewith I think to be bold against some, which think of us as if we walked according to the flesh. For though we walk in the flesh, we do not war after the flesh . . .

2 Corinthians 10:1-3

Paul is addressing an existing problem within the church. Paul is determined to deal with the conflicts existing at Corinth that have not been resolved. If the church would deal with it, Paul wouldn't have to. But if the church doesn't deal with it, Paul must.

Paul understood that some people thought he would walk the way they walked, parading around in the flesh, expressing their thoughts and ideas. However, this was not Paul's style. Instead, he said:

(For the weapons of our warfare are not carnal, but mighty through God to the pulling down of strong holds;) casting down imaginations, and every high thing that exalteth itself against the knowledge of God, and bringing into captivity every thought to the obedience of Christ; and having in a readiness to revenge all disobedience, when your obedience is fulfilled.

Do ye look on things after the outward appearance? If any man trust to himself that he is Christ's, let him of himself think this again, that, as he is Christ's, even so are we Christ's. For though I should boast somewhat more of our authority, which the Lord hath given us for edification, and not for your destruction, I should not be ashamed: That I may not seem as if I would terrify you by letters. For his letters, say they, are weighty and powerful; but his bodily presence is weak, and his speech contemptible. Let such an one think this, that, such as we are in word by letters when we are absent, such will we be also in deed when we are present. For we dare not make ourselves of the number, or compare ourselves with some that commend themselves: but they measuring themselves by themselves, and comparing themselves among themselves, are not wise. But we will not boast of things without our measure, but according to the measure of the rule which God hath distributed to us, a measure to reach even unto you. For we stretch not ourselves beyond our measure, as though we reached not unto you: for we are come as far as to you also in preaching the gospel of Christ: Not boasting of things without our measure, that is, of other men's labours; but having hope, when your faith is increased, that we shall be enlarged by you according to our rule abundantly, to preach the gospel in the regions beyond you, and not to boast in another man's line of things made ready to our hand. But he that glorieth, let him glory in the Lord. For not he that commendeth himself is approved, but whom the Lord commendeth.

2 Corinthians 10:4-18

This is spiritual warfare! This is how to be victorious in life. Wicked men accused Paul of being very bold and boastful in his letters. These wicked men insisted that he was not at all in presence what he was in his letters. These people were trying to belittle Paul, to discredit him, and to dishonor him before the Corinthians. Paul explains that his rule of spiritual warfare and authority within the Corinthian church is simply this: We have a responsibility with you at Corinth because God used us to reach to you; God chose our ministry to bring you the gospel. It was through our labors that God produced this church. It was through our labors that you have been born again. It was through our labors that you were established. We are not going to fool with another man's work, or church, but we are dealing with the church that God developed through us! Our reach is to all those churches that God produced through our ministry and those that seek our assistance.

So Paul says to let them think what they want to think and say what they want to say. But we are coming to Corinth, and when we come, they will find that we are in presence what we are in our letters.

Paul recognized the authority given to him—an authority to deal with situations in the church, to bring judgment, discipline, or rule. He never sought to use his authority to bring destruction, but to profit the body of Christ. Therefore, he tells them to deal with the problems.

I want us to see the struggles that Paul was going through. All of us go through similar struggles, but we have to maintain our victory in Christ. We have to prevent ourselves from acting in the flesh. The flesh is so deceptive because it is going to tell you that your course is spiritual action. We have to be careful that our flesh does not fool us. It is God who commends, and if God does not commend, there is no authority! If God is not backing it, there will be no anointing in it. That is why Paul could say with such confidence that these men can parade themselves all they want to, but God is commending us. God is working with us.

A man walking in the flesh cannot have this confidence, but if we walk in the Spirit, this will always be our testimony. Instead of maintaining a walk in the Spirit, we try to determine how spiritual, holy, and mature in the Lord we are by comparing ourselves with one another. We look at other people, measure their spirituality, and then we place ourselves up to them to see how we measure up.

Paul said that comparing ourselves with ourselves is foolish and a practice he refused to give place to. He knew where he was, and he knew who he was because God commended him as the servant of Christ. This was enough for Paul to act in faith. He refused to let anybody move him out of this line of thinking.

In the church, there are real spiritual battles raging and wicked men who must be overcome! There are men whom we have to deal with in the church, but behind the men are principalities and powers. Our battle is not with the men of the flesh, but with spiritual wickedness. Therefore, the weapons of our warfare are not carnal, but mighty through God to the pulling down of strongholds. Paul is telling us that through God and the weapon that He has given us, we are able to deal with spiritual strongholds in other people's lives, churches, families, homes, and communities.

However, we overlook the most fundamental aspect of where these strongholds must be torn down. Strongholds must be torn down in ourselves. That weapon is most effective in producing our freedom. Until there is freedom in our own spirit, we will never be successful in pulling down strongholds in others!

There are three things that the devil uses as strongholds in a person's life. Paul said the weapons of God are mighty in casting down **IMAGINATIONS**.

Imaginations are reasonings. The word is probably used here in the sense of devices and refers to all the plans of a wicked world, the various systems of false philosophy; and the reasonings of the enemies of the gospel. The various systems of false philosophy were so entrenched that they might be called the stronghold of the enemies of God. The foes of Christianity pretend to have a great deal of reasoning power and rely on that in resisting the gospel (from Barnes' Notes, Electronic Database. Copyright (c) 1997 by Biblesoft).

That is what wicked men were doing in Corinth. They were using their reasonings as to why the people should listen to them and not Paul. Just as there are false philosophies that are enemies of the gospel, there are false philosophies existing within us all, in our flesh. All of my emotions, feelings, and reasonings must be cast down, or else they will be the means by which the devil can operate right out of my life.

A stronghold is a place where the enemy can work, operate, or exist.

The weapons of God are also mighty in conquering **HIGH THINGS EXALTED ABOVE GOD** (and every high thing)— every exalted opinion respecting the dignity and purity of human nature (why I should be this, why I should be that, why I should be treated this way, or why I shouldn't be treated that way). These exalted positions that exist in all our flesh can lead to serious trouble if not cast down. All the pride of the human heart and of the understanding is a stronghold that must be cast down. All human philosophy and opinion is opposed to the knowledge of God. Humanity will always exalt itself into a vain self-confidence. The most veteran of saints will entertain vain and unfounded opinions respecting his own excellence if this stronghold is not cast down! And the babes in Christ will be tempted to determine their own course in Christ, refusing to submit to God in the things He knows they must pass through for their own maturity.

Another weapon the devil uses to build strongholds is **FREE THOUGHTS**.

Free thoughts are those wandering thoughts, thoughts that are not subdued. We would tend to think that this is imagination, but imagination is reasonings—thought-out plans and beliefs that develop into philosophies and courses of action.

Free thoughts are simply thoughts. For example, say you sin against God. Because you sinned, you start thinking. Your thoughts run wild and are not controlled by the Word of God. Because they are unbridled, you begin to question the mercy of God. Your thoughts will not allow you to take refuge in the blood of Jesus. Rather, your thoughts have led you into a realm of feeling—feeling that God is after you now, feeling that God is going to destroy you, feeling that God is finished with you. And then you retreat into depression.

Oh, what a stronghold of the devil! Pastoring for twenty years, I can say that the greatest distress people have been under is that distress that their thoughts produced! Free thoughts create great havoc in our lives. Somebody has said, "Who said worry never works? Rarely does anything I worry about ever happen!"

The apostles said that we are to take every thought captive to the obedience of Jesus Christ. This figure of speech is taken from military conquests where all the defeated foes were led captive by the victorious king. Here we see that Jesus, the conquering King, will lead all of His victims—the strongholds of paganism, and pride, and sin—to their appropriate exile! By Jesus, all of the plans and purposes of the heart, the intellect, and the imagination can be subdued, and the believer can have rest!

If you are not letting Jesus capture your thoughts, you will never have His freedom.

The captives, under His authority, were to be subject to His control.

Every power of thought in the pagan world; all the systems of philosophy and all forms of opinion among people; all the purposes of the soul; all the powers of reason, memory, judgment, fancy in an individual were to come under the laws of Christ. All doctrines were to be in accordance with His will; philosophy should no longer control them, but they should be subject to the will of Christ.

Let a man have free thoughts about not wanting to tithe. Let him build this thought by reasonings: "I don't want to tithe. I don't think I have to tithe!" This is a philosophy of his mind, and if he doesn't let Jesus capture it by submitting to His Word, it becomes an area where the enemy can live and work.

All the plans of life should be controlled by the will of Christ and formed and executed under His control—as captives are led by a conqueror. All the emotions and feelings of the heart should be controlled by Him, and led by Him—as a victor leads a captive.

These three things the devil uses in our lives, churches, and communities to build strongholds. We must give the devil no place; our thoughts must be brought under the control of Jesus. Our exalted opinions of ourselves must be cast down. When we get upset because we are not being treated the way we think we ought to be treated, we are exalting ourselves above God! Whatever is not in agreement with the philosophy of Christ must be cast down. If it is allowed to exist, it will be the place where the enemy can wage successful campaigns in the overthrow of our lives, churches, families, and communities.

Don't give Satan any ground; you know what he is capable of doing. Whatever is not brought under the captivity of Jesus will be brought under the captivity of Satan; you never occupy ground yourself. You are occupied ground, either by the flesh or the Spirit.

Because I am born-again, I choose who will be given the ground. To give ground to the enemy, all I have to do is think like him. I don't have to go to a pagan church to give Satan ground; just thinking like him is enough. Demons are looking for a place to rest. Rest to a demon is darkness. Darkness is anything that is not God! The Word of God is my light. So if I am entertaining a philosophy in my mind that is in disagreement with the Word of God, I am agreeing with devils and creating a place of rest for them! When we listen to gossip, we give place to evil, and that evil will eventually destroy our lives!

I may not always detect the things that exist in you. But I must always, by careful examination, the Word of God, and the aid of the Holy Spirit, detect the things that are in me.

The key to all successful spiritual warfare is revealed in verse 6: "And having in a readiness to revenge all disobedience, when your obedience is fulfilled." There is no aggressive offensive warfare on your part if there is not submission in your heart. There must be freedom in your life.

These strongholds must be torn down in me. I must know and discern if my thoughts are in disagreement with God. I must know if there are philosophies in my life that the Word of God does not approve of. *My freedom does not rest in the absence of strongholds in you, but in the absence of strongholds in me!*

Oh, that we would get principle. How often do believers allow evildoers to cause them to fret? We allow the wickedness in our communities to upset us and steal from us our joy, robbing us of our faith, happiness, and confidence. We await the day of happiness, when everything works out to our liking. Guess what? In this life, it will never be exactly the way you want it!

But true freedom is being victorious even though everything is not going my way. If there are no strongholds in me, I am free! You may choose to keep the strongholds in your life. You may continue in rebellion, and eventually find yourself in a reprobate condition because that is the choice you made. But that choice does not have to rob me of the freedom and victory God has placed before me.

From this place of victory, Satan has no effective weapon against me.

An enemy I had, whose face I strove to know, for hard he dogged my tracks unseen wherever I did go.

My plans he balked, my aims he foiled and blocked my onward way; when for some lofty goal I toiled, he grimly told me "nay."

One night I seized and held him fast, from him the veil did draw;

I looked upon his face at last and lo—myself I saw!"

—Unknown

Paul said he disciplined his body, lest he became disqualified. Great people have all discovered that the first victory they must win is the one with themselves! If I try to use strategies and tactics to get people to do what I want, in the long run, I won't succeed.

The Test of My Spiritual Measure

No greater test comes to a believer than those that involve abuse, rebuke, betrayal, and hurt. In the natural, unresolved emotional pain wreaks havoc on your immune system, cardiac function, hormone levels, and other physical functions.

But in the spirit it simply is a test revealing how much of your old man is still alive!

To be spiritually free of strongholds and successful in spiritual campaigns, I must realize that nothing I face excuses me from 1 Corinthians 13—LOVE!

In the test or trial, I discover my true spirituality. How I am on the outside (in the trial) is what I have been all along on the inside, regardless of how holy and spiritual I considered myself to be! The test reveals you!

The Lesson I Am to Learn

God wants me to learn the cross in its reality, not simply its theology!

God is adamant that I keep a tender and usable heart. It matters not what I do on the outside if on the inside I am fretting, angry, and full of resentment! I can perform in the flesh and act the way I think God would expect, yet my heart may be filled with horrific strongholds! God allows the confrontations so that I may discover how powerful the cross of Jesus is. God wants to demolish the strongholds that may exist in my life. He does not want me to simply "do" what is right; He wants me to "be" right!

The Victory I Am to Have
All spiritual victory is obtained by allowing God to produce a change in you, not that circumstances or others are changing!

Without a change in you:
- You can never escape the devil's reach.
- You can't run. Wherever you go, he has somebody waiting for you there!

With a change in you, you have forever won, though nothing around you has changed.

It's not time that heals, it's insight . . . it's the cross!

I know people who were wounded twenty years ago whose wounds are as fresh today as ever!

"Blessed is the man whose strength is in thee; in whose heart are the ways of them. Who passing through the valley of Baca (WEEPING) make it a well....They go from strength to strength..." (Psalm 84:5-7).

Obviously, not everyone is blessed, nor do they go from strength to strength. The ones who are not blessed and are not strong are those who don't put their trust in God.

BREAKING THE STRONGHOLD
OF REGRET

CHAPTER 2

I want us to savor the freedom we have in Jesus Christ. When the Holy Spirit fills our lives, He breaks strongholds the enemy previously occupied. The Holy Spirit demolishes the enemy's ground by the victory of Jesus' work on the cross. It is so important for us to be filled with the Holy Spirit. If we are not careful, we can neglect the things of the Spirit. By this neglect, we can actually fail to avail ourselves of the liberty and joy that comes from the Spirit of God. This is not to say that you no longer pray or speak in tongues, but that you have lost your shout of victory, your praise, and your liberty! If we do not live in the Spirit, we give room for the enemy to advance. Satan is always after a secure place from which to launch his schemes—a stronghold. Some of Satan's greatest strongholds are religious. He moves empty believers in directions contrary to God, and then causes these victims to believe that this direction is from God, that it is biblical, and that it is truth. In reality, it is a religious stronghold that will bring greater confusion, frustration, and disgrace into our own lives.

These strongholds are manifest within the man by thoughts of failure, unworthiness, and unbelief. He thinks that because he has not performed well, he is unworthy of God's blessings, provision, or leadership. These are religious strongholds because it makes a man think that through the performance of outward things, he can gain God's favor to receive His blessings.

This thinking is contrary to the New Covenant, which testifies that God has promised to bless us through His Son. When we come to God though His Son and not our deeds, works, or performance, we come expecting God to do good things by His grace.

I am pressed to deal with the paralyzing stronghold of regret. Very few people find the courage to move forward once they have experienced significant failure. Perhaps your decisions have tragically altered your life. Now you live with much disappointment. You live with a failure mentality.

Regrets and disappointments come to anyone who has lived. Many have suffered through painful experiences in life because of decisions made, perhaps stepping out of God's will and acting on their own accord. Now they are paying the price. Or perhaps some of the difficult experiences are part of God's course for our lives; God is using them in the end for our own good.

There are painful things that you are going to have to go through. Regret is regret, and it can hurt deeply. But if we cannot get past regret and unmet expectation, we will never have the courage to fulfill God's will for our future; we will not trust Him with it.

Angela married her best friend, so she thought. Before they married, she and Jack could talk for hours on end. But once they said their vows, it wasn't long before he shut down and they became like strangers. Jack was faithful and pleasant, and he worked hard to provide for them, but he was no longer interested in what Angela had done during the day or in what she thought about. Believing that marriage should be more than co-existence, she asked if they could go for counseling. Jack responded, "For what? I don't have a problem. You can go if you want to, but I am fine with the way things are."

Angela felt trapped and hopeless. She had no godly reason to leave the marriage—nor did she have a reason to want to stay in it. But, prone to second-guessing, all she could do was beat herself up for marrying Jack, thinking about what her life might have been if she hadn't married him. Angela always struggled with making decisions, and it seemed that whenever she made one, she lived to regret it. Regret then consumed her so that she couldn't see anything positive or any hope that God would intervene and cause "all things to work together for good." She lived her life looking in a rear-view mirror. She focused on what she had missed and on what might have been if she had done things differently. If only she had known what she knows now!

Angela needs a reality check. All of her regrets would never help her change what had already happened. In fact, they kept her from looking at what she could do to improve her marriage.[1]

Where Do You Live?

People live in this place called regret. Your regret may not be a marriage; perhaps it stems from a job choice or a decision made or friendships you've chosen. So you begin to regret—you regret friends, choices, jobs, and relationships. Now life becomes very painful.

You cannot change what is. What *is*, is. You cannot go back and redo it. However, only you can determine what the rest of your life will be. Do not give what *has been* the power to determine what *will be*. If you trust in the God of redeeming grace, then put your future into His promising hands. In order for that to happen, you must rise up in faith and courage to overcome the fears that cause you to be paralyzed from these awful regrets. You make the choice as to whether you will get past these hindrances or not.

What Does Regret Look Like?

I believe you want to live free. Because you are reading this, you are making the choice to move forward. Therefore, I offer you godly wisdom to deal with regrets and unmet expectations.

First of all, let me explain what unmet expectations are. Expectations are the things I look forward to, things that I want God to do in my life. But they are my expectations. God never told me He would do them; I just presumed He would do them. God's expectation will never disappoint; He has the powerful ability to bring them about!

Our disappointments come because we make decisions without consulting God. Perhaps we thought we consulted God, only to find out later that we actually did not. Then we begin to look back on our life and wonder about the decisions we have made and where we are now.

So strongholds of regrets and unmet expectations look something like this:

"What if I can't hear God?"

"What if God's not leading me?"

"What if my failures have ruined God's plans for my life, and now I must make the best of it?"

Let's say that you have made choices in life that didn't turn out well. Now you become fearful—too fearful to ever make a decision. "I don't know if I should marry this person. What if I marry and it is wrong, like all the other decisions I have made in life?" What would become of your life then? You begin to paint horror pictures of a life that could be. And some people, not because they have made bad decisions, but because they fear regret, end up doing nothing with their lives. There is no achievement, no joy.

Someone once asked, "What guarantee can you give me that my heart will never be broken in love?" The answer, "Never love anybody!" But if I live without loving, then I miss all the blessings of having loved!

Some are so fearful of what could be that they never live. Have you ever met a person who could not make a decision? Everything is hard, stressed. Angela, from our story, second-guessed everything about her life and would beat herself continually over this.

We have to understand that there is a time of grieving and a time for repentance, but there is also a time when we have to say, "Enough with the grieving! Enough with the disappointment! Enough with living in fear. Enough with the "what-ifs!" We must simply recognize that this is what is; I cannot change that, but I can do something about my future.

All of your wishes for what could have been do not change what is—you have to decide to move on. "If only" and "I should have" will dot your thinking and permeate your emotions. Both will kill you. They may kill you slowly, but they will kill you. They will kill your will to keep going, your desire to trust God, and your hope for a future.

As fearful as decision-making can be, it is a necessary part of life. Because decisions greatly affect our lives, we think that we cannot make a mistake.

However, the truth be known, we are not infallible, and we do make mistakes.

I think our real failure is not that we have made bad decisions, but that we don't have faith that our God is our Shepherd; He will lead us into green pastures! Our failure is that we think it is all up to us. We have to get it right. We have to bear all the consequences. If we mess up, we have to make all the corrections. However, I don't have to fear. The Lord, my Shepherd, He will make me lie down beside still waters, maybe not every day, but He will do it! He brings me into green pastures. You know why green pastures are so wonderful? Because you are so tired of the dirt and the dead pastures you had to go through to get to the ones that are green. Sometimes God leads you through a wilderness, or a barren place, not because He is a bad shepherd, but because He is a good Shepherd and He is getting you through this to get you to the still waters!

Just look at God getting Israel through the wilderness. He had to take them through the wilderness to get to the Promised Land. But how they complained. How scared they were to act and possess their promise. Instead of action and faith for the future, they lived in regret: "Oh, that we were back in Egypt!" This regret led to unbelief, which led to a failure on their part to apprehend God's promise for their lives.

Do you see how devastating the stronghold of regrets and failed expectations can be in leading to a failure of faith?

Bad Decisions Are Not the End of Your World

Bad things may happen. However, life is not over; refuse to be enslaved. What could be more tragic than the events that occurred for the first two people in the world? They have children. And in their family they experience the first murder. All Eve knows is that a few days ago, God made a promise that her seed would crush the serpent's head. She was looking for freedom in her son. Her freedom from death and the destruction in her world is now at stake because Cain killed her promise (Abel).

Imagine what went through her mind. This was a painful situation. This was Adam and Eve's hope. Perhaps they thought, *What are we going to do now? Did we miss God? Did we really understand God right?*

And then God moves. It took some time. It did not just happen overnight. However, in about nine months, she gave birth to Seth; God has appointed ANOTHER seed.

So God gives us this record: "And Adam knew his wife again; and she bare a son, and called his name Seth: For God, said she, hath appointed me another seed instead of Abel, whom Cain slew" (Genesis 4:25).

We read in Genesis 5:1-4, "This is the book of the generations of Adam. In the day that God created man, in the likeness of God made he him; Male and female created he them; and blessed them, and called their name Adam, in the day when they were created. And Adam lived an hundred and thirty years, and begat a son in his own likeness, after his image; and called his name Seth: And the days of Adam after he had begotten Seth were eight hundred years: and he begat sons and daughters . . . ."

This describes Adam's generations, and Abel is not mentioned. Did you notice what God did? He gave her "another"!

Another. When God gives you another chance or another relationship or another career, it won't be a continuation of the bad of the past. It will be another, and it will be according to your faith.

What happened to Cain and Abel? They're not mentioned. They didn't make it into the book because Genesis 5 isn't just another chapter of the past. It marks the beginning of something new! Seth is the new legacy by which the promises of God would come.

Consider Job

If there is anyone who could have suffered from second-guessing, regrets, and devastation, certainly Job would top the list. He is qualified to speak to us. At the loss of everything, even the loss of his children, he could have responded by saying, "Oh, that I would have put more soldiers around my camels and sheep; I knew I should have done it! Why didn't I do it?" Perhaps he could have tormented himself over the death of his kids. Perhaps he thought to himself that he didn't offer enough sacrifice: "Just one more lamb would have made the difference!" Job could have tormented himself with "what-ifs."

Instead of second-guessing, he responds this way: "Job arose and rent his mantle and shaved his head and fell down upon the ground and worshipped and said, Naked came I out of my mother's womb, and naked shall I return thither: the LORD gave, and the LORD hath taken away; blessed be the name of the LORD. In all this Job sinned not, nor charged God foolishly" (Job 1:20-22).

To deal with the fear of your tomorrows, you must rest on the providence of God. God rules in life; He is in control! Job rested in God. He couldn't change what had happened, but he could certainly be careful for what would happen. He trusted God. What else is he to do? God gave, and God has taken!

I don't have to worry about my tomorrows and all the decisions "I" have to make because the Lord is my God, and He leads me, protects me, and cautions me. I trust that He will let me know if I am making a decision that is outside of His will. He will warn me and tell me.

Job could not live with questioning how he could have prevented the disasters, or why God did not. You can't live there. It is a valley to pass through, and pass through you must—and quickly!

Job Believed God

Job simply believed that God is in control. There is still grieving in Job's life, as is reflected in Job 29:1-5. "Moreover Job continued his parable, and said, Oh that I were as in months past, as in the days when God preserved me . . ." (Job 29:1-2).

Job is reflecting on the "good ol' days." He used to walk into the gate of the city and the young men would stand to his attention. The old men were silent before him, and the rulers were breathless as Job walked by. It was a day of such honor and prestige, a day of recognition. But now the talk about Job is different. Everybody is talking about how Job must have sinned against God. They are saying that he is not the man they thought he was. Nothing bad like that would happen unless he was a gross sinner. In this hour, no one is standing up for Job; no one admires or recognizes him. They are all suspicious of him.

But Job was not tormented by everyone's suspicions. They made accusations against him, but he simply stood on his integrity and said to them that they were wrong!

Covered in sickness, grieving over his loss, Job reminisces about his past.

Something has happened, and Job is thrown into a horrific situation. Listen to Job as he continues:

> Oh that I were as in months past, as in the days when God preserved me; When His candle shined upon my head, and when by His light I walked through darkness; As I was in the days of my youth, when the secret of God was upon my tabernacle; When the Almighty was yet with me, when my children were about me.
>
> Job 29:2-5

Job remembers the days when his children were around; they shared dinners together, the kids playing. And now those days are all gone.

The sad thing is that many people die here. Though they continue to live "life," they do not continue to live. They can only live in the past for fear of the future. How can I go forward? How can I have more children? Why must I go on when I have had to bury my other children?

Do you know how hard it is to bury your child? Can you fathom the pain in the hearts of parents as they stand over the grave of their baby? Sure, people say that God will take care of them. Yet they stand there thinking that God did not take care of this one.

The difference with Job is that he really knew God! He refused to allow the paralysis of that fear to rule his life; there is more to live for now than there was in the past. So listen as Job gives us some counsel: "After this lived Job an hundred and forty years, and saw his sons and his sons' sons, even four generations. So Job died, being old and full of days" (Job 42:16-17).

After this Job lived! Job LIVED! He lived to see four generations of his children and grandchildren. Then he died, an old man who had LIVED a long "GOOD LIFE!"

Just think if he had given up as a lot of people do. But if you had asked Job at the end of his life how he was doing and what he thought about God and life, he would have said, "I am satisfied! It has been a good life!"

Don't you want to have that testimony in your life? Do you want to let regrets and failures and unmet expectations and bad decisions dictate the result of the rest of your life? I don't think so!

THERE IS LIFE AFTER GREAT LOSS.

Job could have sunk low, sulked, blamed, "Is there anything to look forward to?" You will never know until you go forward and find out! Rather than focus on what might have been, Job focused on reality: God gives. God takes away. God is in control.

Fighting with Him, being angry with Him, speaking out against Him will do no good. With all of his losses, Job's mind wasn't filled with thoughts of what might have been: If only my livestock had been protected better. If only my herdsmen would have survived. If only my children had stayed in their own homes for dinner. "If only . . . ." *Job just didn't go there*. He mourned, he grieved, and he trusted God for the future. As a result, he was able to move on.[2] As well you should. See you in the future!

BREAKING THE STRONGHOLD OF CRITICISM

CHAPTER 3

Being Criticized

Very few people find the courage to move forward once they have experienced the stinging opinions of others who have verbally assaulted them. I am not talking about healthy criticism. I am talking about damaging criticism where strongholds were developed in a person's life. The enemy was able to occupy that ground and bring havoc. These strongholds must be torn down.

Criticism may be a greater stronghold than regrets. Criticism has the ability to strike a person down to where he can hardly rise again. Criticism is when others disapprove of who you are or what you have done. This is very difficult to deal with.

When someone disapproves of you, it is very stinging. It is a pain that lodges deep within your emotions and spirit. It sets you back. You entertain thoughts of quitting, giving up, or, even worse, you begin to live for the person's approval!

You see, when someone criticizes you, you face an emotional meltdown. You have failed in someone's eyes, and now they think ill of you. The simple truth about criticism is that it occurs when you are unable to keep people from thinking that you are what you know you are not. And surely, there are many of us that work to do that.

We know we are fallible, but we want to think we are infallible, and we want everyone else to think we are infallible. Then one day someone looks through all the beautiful images we have created ourselves to be and sees that we are not perfect!

Maybe mean-spirited, they come against you, or perhaps their spirit is right, but their criticism hits us very hard.

She sat across the table from me wringing her hands. "I just want to tell him that he is wrong about me. I need to explain why I did what I did."

The "he" was Sheila's boss, and what she had done was to mix up an important letter with another important letter by putting them in the wrong envelopes and sending them to business associates of her boss—and he was angry. The letters contained information about one of the parties that should not have gone to the other party. Her employer was irate and told Sheila that she was careless and incompetent and that she should be cleaning the office instead of running it. His remarks were cutting and uncalled for, and he said them out of frustration, embarrassment, and anger.

But Sheila took his anger and his comments very person-ally. When she talked with me, she wanted to make an appointment with her boss to explain why she had made the mistake. She was convinced that her explanation would make him understand. She had already told him she was sorry, but she wanted to give him more of an explanation in hopes that he would apologize for what he'd said to her. I told her that I didn't think her explanations would get anywhere with this man. He was upset over what had happened, and he really didn't care what the reason was.

But Sheila couldn't see it that way. She kept saying, "But if he just knew why this whole thing happened, he wouldn't be so angry." As we talked, it was clear that beneath Sheila's need to defend herself was a deep-seated fear that his words might be true—maybe she wasn't a good office manager; maybe she was a careless person. In her mind, if these things were true, then she had no value as a person. She had nothing to offer. She wasn't able to look at what had happened to see if his remarks had any bearing on reality. Even when I would remind her of her excellent performance reviews — both from this same boss and from her staff — she discounted them. She was giving this man way too much power.

Sheila finally wore herself out trying to think up justifications. She just could not keep on doing it. Of course, as could be expected, after she quit trying to prove herself right, as time elapsed, she discovered that the whole incident didn't matter to him as much as it did to her.

You can do everything right all your life, and do one thing wrong, a legitimate mistake that carries a reasonable explanation, and someone comes along and blasts you. They let you have it: They tell you what they think about you, and personally want to offend you. I have seen so many people unable to rebound from this!

We as Christians cannot afford to live with those strongholds in our life, where people's opinions have this type of power over us.[1]

Just one criticism can come and destroy a person's life. Oftentimes criticism is magnified in your mind much more than it is in the minds of those criticizing.

When Your Value as a Person Is Tied Up With a Need to Be Liked, You Won't Be Able to Live Free

I want to emphasize the "need" to be liked. Everyone wants to be liked, but everyone doesn't have a need to be liked. Some people understand that there will be those in the world who don't like them. Now, maybe some of you reading this don't understand that about yourself — yet it is true. The 5 billion people on the planet are not all going to like you — face it!

You think, *But why wouldn't they like me? If they knew me, they would like me! And if that person doesn't like me, I must be an unlikable person.* You know what happens? You have just given your freedom away and made yourself a slave to that one person you know doesn't like you. You are going to live for them, to somehow convince them they should like you. And when you win their approval, you are going to lose someone else's approval!

35

Can you imagine the quality of life you are going to have to look forward to? You can't pull it off. Still there are some people that just feel, "I need you to like me."

If You Lack Knowledge of God's Calling and Word, You Will Not Maintain Freedom

If you don't have knowledge of God's calling on your life or the knowledge of His Word, you will lack freedom, for people will put you in bondage.

If you hate to be criticized and think that criticism is absolutely the worst thing that can happen to you, then it will hurt you deeply and have a negative impact on you. However, if you would simply realize that criticism could be profitable, then you can learn to use it as a factor for personal growth.

Knowing that God loves you and is busy conforming you into the image of Christ, you can learn to use the criticism as a mirror into areas of your life to which you may be blind. Regardless of how the criticism comes, if you will rest on the Holy Spirit, it can be a means of great growth.

Also realize that some of the most powerful truths about yourself will come from those who hate you the most. Unlike your close friends, they are not at all worried about hurting your feelings. Sometimes the criticisms that people give us are truths about ourselves that we don't want to admit, and these oftentimes identify strongholds in our lives that we are not willing to see. If you would bring this criticism to the Holy Spirit, He will use it to bring personal growth.

Never Allow Anyone to Devastate You With His or Her Criticism

If you understand that criticism is something that is going to happen to everyone who lives, then you simply reckon this as one of the events of life. Even though you are being criticized, it doesn't mean that it is true. Give yourself to the Holy Spirit, never to the opinions of man. Give the criticism to the Holy Spirit. If it is true, He will tell you. If it is false, He will also tell you. Then you can move on.

You don't need everyone's approval in your life. To seek only the approval of God and His church is the affirmation we must all pursue.

No one likes criticism, but we must all go through it! In every case, bring it to God. "Lord, this is what they said. You judge the attitude and the spirit in which it was said. But I want you to show me the truth of it. I don't want my heart to be hard. I don't want to be in bondage to their criticism. I don't want to live having to try to please people.

"I want to live to please You. And I want You to be able to say, 'Well done' at the end of my life, even if everyone else called me a fool and a failure. God, I just want to know that I live for Your pleasure and glory."

You Don't Have to Feel Good to Be All Right

One way some suffer with criticism is the compulsive bondage that thinks: *I must be thought of as right, or I can't live with myself. I have to make others understand and acknowledge how right I am.*

No matter what Jesus did, He couldn't please the religious leaders of the day. If He healed, it was on the wrong day. If He ate dinner, it was with the wrong people. If He told the truth about Himself, He was called a liar and a blasphemer. Criticism is a part of life. But just because "they said," it doesn't make it so.[2]

You must never allow criticism to devastate you. There is somebody who is building your life, and that someone is Jesus Christ. You cannot let what a person thinks about you or his opinion of you or how he approaches you about it become the thing that devastates your life or keeps you from moving on.

We believe in a God of grace who is all-powerful; He is able to bring the necessary changes in our lives. And we have to hold on to that belief.

You Can Hear Criticism and Still Fulfill God's Call

Dan was fired from a job he thought he loved. In fact, if you asked him, he did love it. The whole firing episode had been unfortunate and unfair. The company was in a financial squeeze, and Dan and two of his coworkers were let go. They weren't really given explanations for their pink slips, except that their department was costing the firm money instead of producing it. Dan knew that wasn't exactly the truth, but what could he do? The company needed to cut some salaries, and he and his coworkers were among the top-salaried workers. Such is life.

For several weeks he and his wife, Sarah, spent most of their time rehashing what could have been. Dan kept asking, "Why didn't I see this coming?" "I should have done something differently." "I really liked this job. How am I ever going to move up in my career and find a job I like?" They took the layoff personally, saying that Dan's boss had never liked Dan and that if he had really been valued, he would not have been laid off. After all he had done for the company, he still ended up being dumped.

Then six weeks from the time he was fired, Dan almost miraculously had a turnaround in his thinking. He woke up one morning and thought, *This is getting me nowhere.* He made his way into the kitchen and said to Sarah, "Tell me if this is true. Yes, I liked the job. Yes, it was a raw deal to be fired. Yes, I really wish it hadn't happened, but it did, and wishing it hadn't isn't helping us any, is it?" Sarah nodded. "I need to move past this, don't I?" Dan asked. Again, his wife nodded.

Dan had reached a very powerful conclusion: I best get my eyes off what might have been and begin thinking about what can be. Dan decided there was no time like the present to begin looking at the future. He did some serious soul searching about his part in being laid off and about what he really wanted to do. Dan then took responsibility for his own life and moved on. Two months later he was interviewing for a dream job that he never would have even thought about pursuing had he not let go of what might have been.[3]

Even if others realize that you are, at the moment, falling woefully short of God's intentions, God can still make you into a mighty man of faith.

Faith does not exempt you from attack; it prevails over the attack. And how long will the enemy attack you and come against you? As long as you continue to fall into the enemy's hand. When you come to the place in Christ where you refuse to allow these things to beset you, then you have beaten the enemy!

I have seen people become bitter because they were criticized, saying things like, "Can you believe they thought that about me?" But are you not glad that they don't know how you really are? Are you not glad that they don't know what you did in secret, or what you thought in your heart? And we can become so mad, so upset, so offended because they just didn't do it the right way. Well, maybe they didn't do it the right way. And you can run—run to the next church down the street, run to the next city, run to the next state. And guess what? Satan knows your number! He has a critic in every church, every city, and every state. And he will keep you on the run.

You see, these strongholds have to be removed from US so that there is freedom in our lives.

Every Promised Land has giants and strongholds. There is no co-existence; you've got to kill them. As I said earlier, criticism is a means of identifying strongholds in your life. How long will the enemy resist you? Till he knows you will not give up. He hopes you'll get discouraged.

Take what they say to God and ask him if it is true. If what someone has to tell you is painful to hear and you reject it or become defensive, you are in trouble!

It Is Okay for You to Be Wrong, and Make Mistakes, and Be Found With Sin in Your Life

There will be criticism, but it is okay. Your life is not free because no one is criticizing you; your life is free because in spite of all the criticism, even if you have sinned, it is not the end of your life.

I am by no means condoning sin and failure, but there is a remedy for sin—the blood of Jesus Christ. But you get so afraid that someone saw you sin or fail, that somebody saw you lose your temper. Now you feel you cannot ever go back around those good people, musing within, *Oh my, what will they think?* It matters what they think! But what they think is not all-important. If they are really Christians, they will not shun you anyway. And if they are not Christians, please don't let them decide your future. Run to the blood of Jesus; admit it to Him; repent and be reconciled to God.

There are a lot of people who are hurt from their past. Many are afraid of the future because they have watched others make such bad mistakes in the past. They are so scared to move forward, and they end up not moving at all, never living.

Please let the Holy Ghost demolish these strongholds that will slowly demolish your life, marriage, future, and walk with God.

BREAKING THE STRONGHOLD
OF FRETTING

CHAPTER 4

Robert McQuilken, while president of Columbia Bible College, relates the story: A dear Christian mother came at the close of a meeting, and with troubled face and voice cried, "Oh for that life of victory! That is what I need."

She then poured out her story of the trouble in her home because of the unworthy conduct of a young man who had married her beautiful daughter.

"Have you ever read the 37th Psalm?"

Her face lighted up. "That is my favorite psalm. I know it by heart."

"What is the first word of that psalm?" I asked. I expected her to say, "Fret Not." She answered accurately, "Fret."

Would you believe that was the only part of the 37th Psalm she knew from experience? Why? She was fretting much of the time. She repeated the first sentence of the psalm, "Fret not thyself because of evil doers." I asked her who was fretting her. She said it was the young man, and proceeded to tell other things about the troubles in their home.

After repeating the three opening words of this 37th Psalm several times, the meaning of the words "Fret not THYSELF" finally dawned upon her.

"Oh," she cried, "you mean that I'm the one that's doing it, and all the time I thought it was that man."

"Yes, others may be the occasion of our worry, but no one can fret us except we ourselves."

Dr. McQuilken saw in this mother a soul-fixation. Her attention was glued to her problem son-in-law. Only as she deliberately turned her heart toward the Lord was she enabled to turn from "fretting herself."[1]

A person who frets has something worse than worry and anger. He has anger out of control. Though there are many excuses to justify our fretting, the Bible says to fret not yourself!

The dictionary defines fretting as a state of vexation . . . to become chafed or rubbed . . . and to ruffle. Fretting is what one does while lying awake in the night, reflecting on how someone has wronged him. Fretting replays the injustices against you until you become inflamed with anger. By fretting you are obsessed with those who did you wrong because it looks like they are going to get away with it. You want them to pay, to be punished, and this obsession becomes fuel for vindication!

If you are fretting, then realize that you are the one who is causing this agitation and bitterness. You have allowed this hurt to fester, and now you find it very difficult to function.

Fretting can destroy you but never change the problem. Fretting can destroy your home, family, and friendships, but it will never make a bad situation good!

Jan Silvious wisely said that, "Fretting has no redemptive value.

"Fretting begins with an annoyance and irritation and turns into rage . . . a burning anger that sits in the pit of your stomach. It is not an explosive anger, but a gnawing anger . . . a helpless agitation.

"You focus on what is wrong . . . . You think about what is wrong . . . . You plot how to fix those who are wrong."

Sonya['s] . . . father walked away from her mother and her family and was living a life of ease. This rubbed a sore into Sonya's soul. She seemed to be angry, hurt, and obsessed all at the same time. Every conversation with her ended in a statement about her father's selfish and despicable behavior. How on earth could he get away with having all the money he wanted while her mother and family were barely able to make ends meet? Sonya had tried her best to get her father to change by telling him how his reprobate behavior was creating such a hardship on the family. But he was unmoved, letting Sonya know that he couldn't care less about her mother's tears. The fact that his family was barely able to keep a roof over their heads and food on the table meant nothing to him.

When Sonya wasn't able to convince her father that he was wrong, it only made her fret more. After all, what her dad had done was wrong! He was wrong! Sonya made sure that everyone knew the truth: Her dad was wrong! But fretting over the fact that her dad was wrong—and getting away with it—did not change the facts. . . . It made her unhappy, unpleasant to be around, and unable to go on with her life.[2]

How to Stop Fretting: Trust in the Lord

Some of the reasonings one may use to justify fretting go something like this. The unrighteous person doesn't know God. He doesn't have a relationship with the Lord. Therefore, it is up to me. I have to do it, to convince him, to make him realize how bad and wrong he is.

The Bible says that if I want to be free, then I must trust in the Lord. Luther dealt with fits of depression. One day a friend said to him,

> Our Lord in heaven is looking down and probably thinking, "What shall I do with this man Luther? I have poured My mercies upon him and given him many gifts and much grace, yet he will despair of My goodness."

Luther was shaken. Luther later helped another fretting friend who said the devil was buffeting him. Luther said,

> The devil can do that in a masterly way; otherwise he would be no devil. You come to me, dear friend, and believe that I can surely comfort you through God's Word, and that

is good. But if you expect good from me, what may you not expect from Christ who died for you? Look up to Him who is ten thousand times better than I.[3]

Corrie Ten Boom gives the true life account of seeing horrific things done to friends and family while suffering at a concentration camp in Germany. The Germans stripped the women and drove them out into the snow. They took delight in torturing prisoners. Corrie recognized the bitterness invading her heart. She also realized that there was nothing she could do to change the Germans, but there was something she could do about herself. She prayed, "Lord, let me realize the freedom of Christ that is beyond this." That is all she asked. The Lord responded, "You have been looking at the Germans. Don't rely upon any of them to do right, but rely on me to do good!" She decided to trust the Lord and take Him at His word, even when feelings and circumstances would make it so hard to maintain her view of God. She felt God was saying, "When you get out of this concentration camp, and you are free of the Germans, you must be sure that your heart is free as well. You can be let out of this camp and still be in the greatest prison of all."

The thing that is going to destroy your life is the thing that you allow into your heart.

Delight Yourself in the Lord

Fretting occurs when it appears justice has failed; it appears the wicked are successfully persecuting the righteous. But even here we have a scriptural answer, "The righteous are going to inherit the earth and the wicked will be cut off" (Psalm 37:28-29).

Delight yourself in the Lord because of the promises of God. Build your world and perspective in God. Bring all your heart rest and happiness on the Lord alone and His good nature. Do not let your joy become dependent on people or circumstances. Never let people have that much power over your delight and joy by thinking, *I'll be happy today if it goes my way. I'll be happy today if the people who cause me trouble will do right to me today, if the people who are wrong will admit they are wrong.*

You are putting too much stock in the nature of people and their instability to provide you a joy in the Lord.

The only one worthy and able is the Lord. Delight in Him! Come to God and say, "Lord, I know there will be some difficult things today, and perhaps some tribulation may come my way, but it is enough for me if you are the delight of my life. I am going to purpose in my heart that my joy will not be a pleasant home or family or circumstances, but my joy will rest in you, the living God."

Miserable things may be happening today, but I am glad I am going to heaven, and soon I will see God. Injustice is everywhere. The wicked are prospering, but I have a God who will feed me, who has prepared for me everlasting delights in His home. You may have riches today, and tomorrow they can be gone. I have God today, and I'll have God tomorrow! All I know is this: I was young, and now I am old, and I have never seen the righteous forsaken nor their seed begging for bread. That is my joy and my delight! God will take care of me. When that is the whole source of my joy, I will be joyful! But if I cause my happiness to be contingent upon people or circumstances, then I will be as disturbed as a leaf in a hurricane!

Commit Your Way to the Lord

In Psalm 37, the Holy Spirit deals with injustice and the prosperity of the wicked. He deals with people who don't know the Lord and with those who do—people I will fret over. When God's Word says to commit my way to the Lord, it means: How am I going to handle this? What am I going to do with what I know is going on? When I am determined to commit my way to the Lord, it means that I cannot determine anybody else's behavior. I cannot make anyone else act appropriately. I cannot make anyone repent. I cannot make people do wrong or do right. I can manipulate and abuse, but if they don't want to respond accordingly, I cannot make them do it. However, I can do something about my way! If there are people I am surrounded by, and they want to take the way of unrighteousness, then that is the way they have chosen. But I will commit my way to the Lord. Jesus taught us what this means. It means that I am to love my enemies

To bless those who curse me . . .
To do good to them that hate me . . .
To pray for those who use and abuse me!

You are to walk in a way that any child of God would walk. You don't just love those who love you, for how would you be different from any other pagan in the world? The publicans do this! You are to be perfect because your Father in heaven is perfect!

This is the "way" you commit. It is the way of righteousness, the way of Christ. I am not going to be bitter. I am not going to fret. I am not going to be angry. I am not going to sulk. I am not going to allow strongholds to be built in my life. I choose the way of meekness . . . of humility . . . of prayer . . . of blessing others . . . of doing good to others when they have done wrong to me. I am committed to this way, and I am trusting God to give me the spirit and strength to walk in this way.

Rest in the Lord

If you want to be free from fretting, then you must REST in the Lord! If you are fretting, then you are not resting.

Psalm 37 tells us to rest in the Lord. I would like to relate this to Philippians 4, where Paul said he learned to be content in whatever situation in which he found himself. He was abused, and sometimes he was treated well. Sometimes he was hungry, and other times well fed. There were times he was poor, and other times wealthy, but the key is that he learned to be content in any situation!

I believe Paul learned contentment by this process: First, he learned how to deal with worry through prayer. He took his worries and handed them over to God by praying. He learned that by prayer and supplication, with thanksgiving, he didn't have to be anxious for anything. The peace of God that passes all understanding kept his heart and mind in Christ Jesus. This was experience for Paul. He didn't read that from Peter or the Psalms; he experienced this in his own life!

Paul suffered all types of abuses and stresses, and mostly from church members! Everywhere he went, he faced troubles. So what is he to do with all this worry? He cannot give it to Timothy; he can't handle it. So what did Paul do? He prayed! He called upon the Lord, "Take these cares, take these anxieties, take these things that are causing me to be stressed out, and I thank you for taking them, and I thank you for your faithfulness, and I thank you for your goodness, and I am going to rejoice in everything." And he learned that God took them.

Secondly, he learned to think right, to set his mind. People who fret are those who allow their minds to dwell on the wrong things. They think on injustice. They plot how they can convince and manipulate to make it right. They think about how much they hurt, how so-and-so hurt their feelings. They think about how they were abused or taken advantage of; they dwell on their wounds.

The Bible says that whatsoever is pure, lovely, good, virtuous, and full of praise—think about these things. I choose what I think about. I am not going to waste my time thinking about how people hurt me. I have a natural tendency to do that, but as a born-again man, I don't have to do that anymore!

Third, Paul learned to follow godly leadership. Paul said the Philippians were to follow what they have seen in him. He told them to practice it. Practice the truth; don't just agree with it, do it! Don't just agree with prayer—pray! Don't try to think on what is right, THINK ON WHAT IS RIGHT! And likewise, commit your way to godly leadership and practice the truth.

Please understand that if you are ever going to be content, then you must learn how to have contentment. I am not saying that God cannot give us contentment and rest to our souls, but the apostle Paul had to learn contentment. That is something we are all going to have to learn if we desire to live contented. Paul's summation of the lesson learned and contentment gained was, "I can do all things through Christ who strengthens me." He learned that. It wasn't a memory verse stuck on his refrigerator. When he was beaten, he got up from it. When he was threatened not to preach anymore, he got up and preached in His name. He realized he was doing things by the life of Jesus, which was in Him. He knew that, by Christ, he could overcome all things; he could be delivered from persecution. Like Paul, I can be free. I will not be ruled by anything other than the Holy Ghost.

Lay it down—don't blame, don't fight to be understood, or even argue for your way to be seen as right. Let it go!

Wait Patiently for the Lord

If you have been fretting and you are not seeing things change, be patient and wait on the Lord.

Say, "Enough!" to the anger and get over it! There has to be a point in every day where I stop my anger. I must not let the sun go down on my anger, or else I give place to Satan.

Yes, they were rude to me and treated me unfairly, but it is not written that life will be fair. Furthermore, this will not be the end of my world.

There are going to be things done to me that are unfair, but I will determine by faith in Christ that none of these things will be the end of my life. It might hurt me; I'll get over it! It might make me angry; I'll give it to God. It might bring worry into my life; I'll give it to God. But by God, it will not destroy me, and it will not be the end of my life. I refuse to allow that to happen. I will not fret myself because of evildoers. I don't have to, and neither do you.

I invite You, Lord, to look into my heart. Look deep within my heart. Often I think I am over something that still remains lodged within. Lord, my heart has hurt. The fretting, bitterness, and anger are there to meet You. It is written all over my attitude, life, and behaviors. I don't want this to rule over me; I want to be free. I don't want there to be strongholds in my life. I ask, by the weapons of our warfare, which are mighty through You to the pulling down of this stronghold, by the truth that comes to set me free, set me free, God! Make me willing to commit my way to You, to trust You for the power to walk in that way, and to agree with You as to the way I should take. Give me the disposition I should have, the life I should live, the attitude I should display. Let me agree with You about what that is and trust You and receive from You the power of the Spirit to walk in Your way. I thank You that my life and happiness do not depend on what others do or don't do to me, but on your faithfulness and love for me!

BREAKING THE STRONGHOLD OF UNFORGIVENESS

CHAPTER 5

How can I forgive people who keep hurting me? The Bible is clear: Unforgiveness in the life of a believer will bring personal bondage and torment of horrific proportions! A root of unforgiveness is able to spring up into all sorts of other evils, such as bitterness, wrath, and emulations.

Forgiveness is not easy; it is divine. The ability to forgive is not something fallen man is naturally endowed with. Sin has killed that noble quality in man. God alone is able to forgive, and because He lives in us, He gives us the grace to forgive.

Though it often is considered an emotion, forgiveness is an act of the will. If we treat forgiveness as an emotion (I feel like forgiving you), then what about those days we don't feel like forgiving? If our forgiveness depends on how we feel, then we are going to allow ourselves to be the rule as to what we should do: Today I feel like forgiving you, so I am going to.

The Bible brings us out of this worldly, carnal thinking and tells us that forgiveness is the course of action we must be committed to in the will and in the heart. By faith we walk in action. The reason we forgive is that we have been forgiven. Jesus says this is the way the people of His kingdom act.

One of the real difficulties we wrestle with in forgiving others is opening ourselves up to being hurt again! When you are willing to forgive, that means you are making yourself vulnerable again to more pain. Your emotions are at risk; you face the possibility of being bruised again. It is natural to want to withdraw from someone who has hurt us. But in forgiveness, we understand that withdrawing is not always the proper action to take. Withdrawal was not God's response to our offenses!

To forgive, we must not succumb to our need for self-justification. We have to be careful that we are not occupied with making ourselves look good and the other look bad. To forgive properly, I must be willing to let "it" ("it" being the problem that has come between us) go and not manipulate in an effort to make this person understand the problem the way I understand it.

Forgiving people who have accidentally hurt us comes fairly easy. We understand that it was an accident. We know they didn't mean to do it. They don't hurt us habitually. We understand they may be going through something; maybe they didn't really mean what they said; maybe they didn't really understand what their actions did to me. So yes, I am willing to forgive them. I know that it is not something they do to me often, and I know they are sincere and love the Lord. We understand that we have been forgiven by God; therefore, we are able to give them that forgiveness.

But there is another situation. Matthew records a conversation between Jesus and Peter:

> Then came Peter to him, and said, Lord, how oft shall my brother sin against me, and I forgive him? till seven times? Jesus saith unto him, I say not unto thee, Until seven times: but, Until seventy times seven. Therefore is the kingdom of heaven likened unto a certain king, which would take account of his servants. And when he had begun to reckon, one was brought unto him, which owed him ten thousand talents. But forasmuch as he had not to pay, his lord commanded him to be sold, and his wife, and children, and all that he had, and payment to be made. The servant therefore fell down, and worshipped him, saying, Lord, have patience with me, and I will pay thee all. Then the lord of that servant was moved with compassion, and loosed him, and forgave him the debt. But the same servant went out, and found one of his fellowservants, which owed him an hundred pence: and he laid hands on him, and took *him* by the throat, saying,

Pay me that thou owest. And his fellowservant fell down at his feet, and besought him, saying, Have patience with me, and I will pay thee all. And he would not: but went and cast him into prison, till he should pay the debt. So when his fellowservants saw what was done, they were very sorry, and came and told unto their lord all that was done. Then his lord, after that he had called him, said unto him, O thou wicked servant, I forgave thee all that debt, because thou desiredst me: Shouldest not thou also have had compassion on thy fellowservant, even as I had pity on thee? And his lord was wroth, and delivered him to the tormentors, till he should pay all that was due unto him. So likewise shall my heavenly Father do also unto you, if ye from your hearts forgive not every one his brother their trespasses.

Matthew 18:21-35

One of the great characteristics of Jesus' kingdom and qualities of God is forgiveness. I am very glad that God is willing to forgive seventy times seven times. I don't know how many times I have played the fool before God. In altars I have promised God never to hurt Him again, only to be caught repeating my foolish actions.

So Where Do We Draw the Line? Do We Continue to Forgive and Get Hurt Again?

Listen to Peter's question. "How often shall my brother sin against me, and I forgive him?" Jesus said that every time somebody comes to you asking for forgiveness, you must forgive him in your HEART!

Peter is not asking about people who might hurt him on rare occasions. Peter is asking about forgiving somebody who is hurting him over and over! Peter is willing to forgive him seven times. But Jesus is saying, "No, Peter. Don't keep a record." Forgive him from your heart every time your forgiveness is sought.

If you don't forgive FROM YOUR HEART, then the king will hand you over to be tormented until your debts have been paid.

Does God really expect me to forgive persons who willfully, intentionally, and successfully offend me again and again? And how can we just forgive persons who don't even know that what they are doing to us is wrong?

To put it in perspective, Jesus told us to remember how the King has forgiven us! We are the recipients of unlimited mercy and grace; by what right do we have to withhold it from others?

There Are Three Types of People Who Will Hurt You Over and Over Again That You Must Forgive

One type is the unrepentant.

We understand from 2 Corinthians 7 that not all sorrow is godly sorrow. There is a worldly sorrow that leads to death. There are a lot of people who are sorry. They are going to come and say they are sorry, yet they have never really repented. There will be people in our lives who hurt us repeatedly and have no repentance. They might express sorrow, but this is not repentance.

Our heart has to have a disposition to forgive all people. The Bible tells us, "For God so loved the world that He gave His only begotten Son that whosoever believes in Him should not perish but have everlasting life." We understand that God sent His Son into the world to die for us while we were yet sinners! We were God's enemies! We rejected His Son! We rejected His offer of salvation! We pierced Him with our sins. Jesus came into a world knowing that narrow is the way, and few there be that find it. He knew that many would take the broad way to destruction.

This means that Jesus loved everybody, and the heart of God is to forgive. His desire is to take every enemy and, by the offering of His Son, bring that enemy to a place of reconciliation. This is what God wants. God knows how we hated, blasphemed, and trashed His laws, but He still acted to redeem us!

Although God has the desire to forgive all, most people have never experienced the forgiveness of God. They have never entered into a relationship with Him because they were unrepentant! They didn't want it. God was willing to pay a price for the relationship to be restored, but many were not willing, or desiring, to have a relationship with God. The heart of God is not bitter or desiring to condemn.

So when the Bible says that we are to forgive those who have offended us and wounded us, it is for our freedom. Jesus told Peter that this is necessary if we are to live a life free from torment and suffering. The effects of unforgiveness are disastrous in our homes, relationships, and personal joy.

By the grace of God, we can have a heart of forgiveness toward our greatest enemies. If you are praying for that person to be destroyed, to die, to go to hell, your heart is in a precarious state. How could we want anybody to go to hell? Are you not glad that God doesn't want you to go to hell? If we are praying for their pain and suffering within our hearts, then we are probably suffering far more than we want them to!

If someone in our life is hurting us often, then this is the course of action that the Lord has shown us:

Go to him and explain the offense. Let him know the damage his actions have brought into the relationship. Explain why his actions have discouraged any type of relationship.

God clearly showed us how we failed and offended Him. With the same Spirit that Jesus came into the world with, go to him and say, "I am willing to establish a relationship with you in spite of all of this. But your actions, which are these, have caused great pain. I want you to know that anytime you want to make this right and are willing to see the damage you are doing to my life, I want you to know that my desire is to forgive you. By the grace of God, I want that. But as long as you have it in your mind to be my enemy and wound and hurt me, we just cannot have a relationship."

Then leave it with the Lord. You have done what is required of you. You are not the Holy Spirit, and you cannot make a person do right. Find your contentment in being right in your heart before God. Take advantage of your opportunity to show Christ to that individual.

Another type is the falsely repentant.

The falsely repentant consistently hurt you and then seek forgiveness with no intent to change. These can be the worst, for they are evil and deceitful, for they say to your face they are sorry but don't mean it. This will come from the religious, who try to deal with their guilt by saying they are sorry without ever having a change of heart.

Now, the Bible warns us about judging another man's heart. We are not able to discern our own heart, much less that of another. So how do I know if their repentance is sincere? John the Baptist helps us. He said, "Bring forth therefore fruits worthy of repentance, and begin not to say within yourselves, We have Abraham to *our* father: for I say unto you, That God is able of these stones to raise up children unto Abraham" (Luke 3:8).

Examine the fruit of a person's life. John is saying, "You are coming to me and want to be baptized, so let me see the sincerity of your repentance by the fruit of your actions."

Please understand, I realize that we can become exasperated when a person is betraying and hurting us over and over again. Do you keep taking it because he says he is sorry? "Because I am a Christian, I have to forgive them when they ask me, but when does this stop? When can I be relieved from this pain they cause me? What do I do?" This is where a lot of people fail to go forward with forgiveness.

God knows the heart of man. When a man sins against God and goes to Him for forgiveness, God knows if he is sincere; God knows his heart. However, as men, we do not know if he is sincere. There is a difference between forgiving a person and trusting a person.

If a person comes to us for forgiveness, then we must, from the heart, forgive him. Now, what do I mean by that forgiveness? I am not God; I cannot say, "I will trust you with this again." But I can say, "I am willing to trust you again. So you bring fruit that will reveal the sincerity of your repentance. Let me see by the actions of your life that you are indeed serious. And if that fruit is obvious, then I will trust you again. I will help and encourage you, but I will be cautious because I want to see fruit."

We want to be peacemakers, but we are not called to be doormats for hypocrites and liars! For example, someone comes into the church. In his past, he was guilty of child molestation, but in the church, he is gloriously born-again. His whole life has changed, and he now wants to walk in that new life. He desires to be forgiven for the life he once lived in. We are to forgive him, but we must exercise caution over the weakness that is still in his flesh. Now he wants to become involved in the church and request a position of working with the children. It would not be a lack of forgiveness to deny him that position! If he is truly born-again, he would not want to put himself into such a compromising position ever again!

The next type is the weakly repentant.

This person is very sincere in his repentance, but he is very weak. He just can't get past this besetting sin. He is sincere, but is weak and truly broken by the damage he causes.

This person will come crying and broken about what he did. The problem is when a person comes to us with such brokenness and sorrow, we feel so sorry for him that we don't even bring up the cause of offense. We don't want him to hurt and suffer in sorrow any more than he is doing right now. However, if we want this problem to end, then we must deal with it. If you want to prevent repeated offenses against your life, take the opportunity to discuss why such offenses occur and how they hurt you.

When we come to God in brokenness, He deals with us. He wants us to confess our sins. Why? Because it helps us confront the ugly things that we are and the ugly deeds we have done.

Now, your point in dealing with them is not to condemn or add sorrow to sorrow. The motivation is healing.

If this person is constantly hurting you and you say, "I cannot take it anymore," then think about what limit you would want God to put on forgiving you. Jesus taught us, in prayer, that we are to ask for the "forgiveness of our debts as we forgive those who are indebted to us."

According to the parable in Matthew, when you have been forgiven by the King, then you must return the kindness to others. No one has committed sin against us that rivals the sins we have committed against God, yet He forgives us!

Do unto others as you would have them do unto you. I don't want to put any limit on God's forgiveness to me. So when I discern that my heart is putting limits on forgiving, I must be honest about it. Well, maybe I can't take anymore! But in faith I can do all things through Christ who strengthens me! I can't take it anymore, but God can give me the grace to take it over and over.

I may not have a close relationship with this person. However, I can see the sincerity and desire he has, and thus encourage him and help him.

> If I say yes, I forgive, but I cannot forget, as though the God who twice a day washes all the sands on all the shores of all the world could not wash such memories from my mind, then I know nothing of Calvary love.
>
> —Amy Charmichael

In forgiveness, let him know, "You don't owe me anything. I am not requiring you to perform for me at all."

When looking for fruit, be careful to realize that we do not determine what the fruit of repentance is; that would make us manipulators! What we want to see is the fruit of the Holy Spirit in the lives of those who have offended us. It is the Word of God that defines the repentance in a person's life. Accept him in fellowship. Accept him in love.

Being a Christian does not exempt us from offending others, or being offended by others. Because a person sins against me, it does not mean that he is not a believer. Someone is going to let you down. Someone is going to break a confidence, and you must have a heart of forgiveness. If you don't have a heart of forgiveness, there will be a stronghold in your life. It will bring torment and destroy the healthy relationships you once enjoyed. You cannot afford to allow this torture to come upon you!

Now, forgiveness never condones sin! As Christians, we must have deep conviction when we transgress against God and His children. Paul said to the Ephesians,

> Be ye therefore followers of God, as dear children; And walk in love, as Christ also hath loved us, and hath given himself for us an offering and a sacrifice to God for a sweetsmelling savour. But fornication, and all uncleanness, or covetousness, let it not be once named among you, as becometh saints; neither filthiness, nor foolish talking,

nor jesting, which are not convenient: but rather giving of thanks.

Ephesians 5:1-4

We have a standard. We do not make excuses for sin: "Oh well, they are just trying to make it." That is not Christianity! Christianity is not defined by a person's sin; it is defined by the victory of the life of Jesus over all sin in the person's life! If there is a person in your life, in your church, who says he is a Christian and yet is sinning against you, then deal with it! Bring the Word of God into the situation. Let the Holy Spirit bring true conviction into his life so that he has such great sorrow that it leads him to repentance!

Regardless of what course of action others take, be sure that your actions are faithful to Christ. To help you keep yourself in the proper place before God and to maintain a pure and tender heart, I offer the following exhortation.

Love at all times.
Proverbs 17:17 reads, "A friend loveth at all times, and a brother is born for adversity."

Be faithful when others are going through adversity. Remember, how do you want God to treat you?

Stick with him.
Proverbs 18:24 reads, "A man that hath friends must shew himself friendly: and there is a friend that sticketh closer than a brother."

People come to church on the basis of receiving God's acceptance. It is a shame if His people do not give that same virtue. It gives me joy to know He is still helping me.

Be faithful in wounding him.
Proverbs 27:5-6 states, "Open rebuke is better than secret love. Faithful are the wounds of a friend; but the kisses of an enemy are deceitful."

What are the kisses of an enemy? It looks something like this: Say you know something is going on in your life. You approach somebody in the church and confess, "I just feel so horrible about

myself and how I behave. I am so disappointed about my witness."
Then that person just "kisses" it: "Oh, I think you are wonderful.
You know everybody has problems, and nobody is perfect. But I
just think you are wonderful. You are not so bad. Look at what other
Christians do."

Sadly, many struggling believers think that those who give these
"kissy" responses are their true friends. These "kissy" enemies tell
us what we want to hear. They give us this warm feeling we long for.
They give us a false sense of relief from the guilt of our crimes.

But faithful are the wounds of a friend. The wounds of a friend
look something like this: "You know what? You are right! What you
did is horrible. Your behavior is wrong. You did sin against God.
You are in disobedience to God's Word." And that type of honesty
in friendship hurts. But those wounds are faithful.

You are going to be hurt, but that gives you no excuse to run,
withdraw, become rude, or disassociate yourself as a friend. Never
allow your heart to become hard or full of anger and self-pity. Most
people never recover from a hardened heart! Your forgiveness to
them is not a guarantee they will ever change; to change them is not
your job. You cannot change them, but you can forgive them.

BREAKING THE STRONGHOLD
OF PAST SIN

CHAPTER 6

One of the greatest hindrances in my relationship with God is the reality of my past sins. The sins of my past are things that often rob me of the confidence that I could have before God. Satan also attempts to use these against me. If I am not careful, they can become a stronghold in my life, causing me to suffer defeat in areas where I should have victory.

The Reality of Sin as a Stronghold in Our Lives

I don't think anyone would argue with the fact that personal sin can bring strongholds in a person's life. Solomon said, "For the ways of man *are* before the eyes of the LORD, and he pondereth all his goings. His own iniquities shall take the wicked himself, and he shall be holden with the cords of his sins. He shall die without instruction; and in the greatness of his folly he shall go astray" (Proverbs 5:21-23).

Nothing is more tragic in the believer's life than being over-taken in sin. It impairs his relationship with God. However, God has provided a remedy for the believer's sin. By the blood of Jesus, the believer has access to forgiveness and reconciliation with God.

In an age that often speaks of positives, the knowledge of sin and how believers should deal with sins has become a rare topic for discussion. First of all, no one likes to admit to sinning. And because it is a "sin" for believers to sin, the topic of a believer repenting is not popular. Though the topic is not popular, the need for believers to find freedom and joy in the presence of God is necessary today.

As believers, we have to deal with the actual times in our life when we have fallen into sin.

Sin is poisonous and destroys the whole quality of life. Sin brings death, doom, and despair. All have suffered from it. The inner life disintegrates when sin is allowed in. The flesh lusts after forbidden pleasure; the soul is brought under the dread of offending God. The sense of judgment weighs heavy upon the sinner's head. The person who has sinned is in pain and sorrow. He is naked and barren. He is heavy-laden. He is dirty and cannot wash clean. He feels that he cannot escape; his sin is always before him. His sin argues against expecting blessings. His sin stands as evidence as to why God cannot use him. His sin prevents him from intimacy with God. The fallen believer is robbed of joy and gladness. His heart is mercilessly assaulted.

How Does God Accept Us?

For some who may be dealing with sin in their lives, it is vital that they believe that Jesus has come to give them liberty. Liberation is the working of the cross. "It is for freedom that Christ has set us free." It is essential that you understand what makes you acceptable in the eyes of God.

The world system says you're valuable because of what you "do." Therefore, you try harder. Until you know that God loves you apart from what you "do," you will stumble along believing your acceptance with God is performance-based.

God is concerned with how we live, but only as it is a result of the work of the cross. It is not your effort through self to walk in the light with God. It is not your performance and the fulfilling of legal demands that gives you the privilege of enjoying God's presence. This idea causes many Christians to lose their intimacy with God. They try so hard and become so religious. God wants us to live by the power of the cross, not in the power of our will!

God has invited us into His presence not because of what we do, but because of what Jesus has done! John said:

That which was from the beginning, which we have heard, which we have seen with our eyes, which we have looked upon, and our hands have handled, of the Word of life; (For the life was manifested, and we have seen *it*, and bear witness, and show unto you that eternal life, which was with the Father, and was manifested unto us;) That which we have seen and heard declare we unto you, that ye also may have fellowship with us: and truly our fellowship *is* with the Father, and with his Son Jesus Christ. And these things write we unto you, that your joy may be full. This then is the message which we have heard of him, and declare unto you, that God is light, and in him is no darkness at all. If we say that we have fellowship with him, and walk in darkness, we lie, and do not the truth: But if we walk in the light, as he is in the light, we have fellowship one with another, and the blood of Jesus Christ his Son cleanseth us from all sin. If we say that we have no sin, we deceive ourselves, and the truth is not in us. If we confess our sins, he is faithful and just to forgive us *our* sins, and to cleanse us from all unrighteousness. If we say that we have not sinned, we make him a liar, and his word is not in us.

1 John 1:1-10

Notice what happens to those who enter this fellowship with God. Sin is dealt with in their lives: "The blood of Jesus . . . cleanseth us from all sin." No one will be as conscious of sin as the man who walks in the light. Everyone who has truth in him will know that he has sin in him. What, then, is he to do? He must confess his sin!

This Passage Is for Believers

We have to understand the context of this passage from 1 John. John is not dealing with the lost. He is talking about people who are in fellowship with God. They are walking in the light with God. As they are walking in the light with God, dark things in them are exposed. The believer is going to realize shortcomings in his life, shortcomings that God is sanctifying him from. If there is truth in you, you will discern the reality of sin.

Though you are not perfect and fall short of the mark God has, if you stay in the light, then you have fellowship with God. In this fellowship, God is cleansing you from sins. For example, God reveals some element of pride. You realize it because you are in the light. Your responsibility is to confess that sin of pride to God. If you refuse to confess and continue to walk in that prideful state, you no longer walk in the light that He has given.

You are now walking in your own light. This does not mean that you are lost. It means that the intimacy of God's presence is broken because of a refusal to confess what the Holy Spirit has revealed in your life. However, when you confess it, God cleanses, and you continue to enjoy His fellowship. Then the Holy Spirit puts His finger on other things in your life: things such as lust, greed, or covetousness. As long as you walk confessing these things to the Lord, you enjoy the communion of His joyful presence and the power of His blood to cleanse.

When a people cry for revival, they are, more often than not, a people who belong to God. There are some who, even while belonging to God, have lost the intimacy of God's presence through a lack of confession. The Holy Spirit has been dealing with them about certain issues within their lives or church. Because they have neglected walking in the light of God's fellowship, they have not sensed His dealings with them. Therefore, they have not been experiencing the joy of confession, cleansing, and sanctification.

Finally, they come to the place where they are longing for God's presence again. They know something is wrong: They are not affected by God's Word. They don't enter into the worship like they used to when the singing would start. They now fall asleep in church, whereas they never used to. There used to be a fire in the soul, but that has waned. All this happens because God put His finger on something in their lives, and they said, "No!" God is going to let them know that until they confess that thing; He cannot walk with them as though everything is fine.

So the closer any Christian gets to God, the more he is going to realize the depravity of his nature, the sin that is in his flesh. Any person who walks in the light realizes that apart from God's fellowship, he would run back into darkness and sin. A person who says he has no sin deceives himself, and the truth is not in him. The person in grave danger is not the one who is walking in the light and is convicted about shortcomings in his life—his prayer life, or Bible study, or home life. A Christian who thinks he is perfected and has no need for the work of sanctification is in grave danger! If you are in the light, with a God in whom there is no darkness, then He will expose the darkness in your flesh.

So the question to answer is, What do we do with those sins that God is convicting us of?

The Ground of Forgiveness—Breaking Strongholds

C.H. Mackintosh wisely teaches that three things have to be dealt with for the stronghold of sin to be demolished: The justice of God has to be satisfied; the conscience of the sinner has to be at peace; and the argument of Satan has to be silenced. How is all this to be done? The ground of forgiveness is the blood of Jesus, the cross of Jesus.

At Calvary, God took every sin and laid it upon His Son. When you come to the cross as a sinner, He takes all of Christ's righteousness and wraps you up in it. From that point, He deals with you in the covenant relationship of atonement.

Jesus loves you unconditionally and is committed to working with you. And He doesn't condemn you while He is doing it. God is faithful to the justice He meted out on Christ to forgive and cleanse you! He is not doing it because we deserve it. He is doing it because Jesus His Son suffered at the hand of His justice, and so God faithfully forgives and cleanses all who confess their state to Him.

Consider the parables of the Lost Sheep, the Lost Coin, and the Prodigal Son. When the man finds his sheep, what does he do? Does he complain of all the troubles the sheep caused and commence to drive the sheep home before him? Ah, no. He lays it on His shoulders. How? Complaining of the weight or the trouble? No. He carries it—rejoicing! Isn't that a wonderful picture of God? He puts you on His shoulders—rejoicing!

And consider the woman. She lights a candle and seeks her lost coin. How? Does she search with weariness and indifference? No! She searches diligently.

Notice the joy of the prodigal's father. He is happy that his son is returning home. He is not happy with the things his son has been involved in. But he is happy that his son has repented and has returned home.

And so God is not happy with the things you have been involved in. However, He is happy when you repent and return home!

God is faithful and just to forgive us our sins and cleanse us. Now, he says faithful and just. Why does he not say gracious and merciful? Because the entire question of sin was settled by the death of Christ, who is now up in heaven as the righteous Advocate. The matter of removing sin is not a matter of grace and mercy; it is a matter of legalities and justice. Therefore, a just God dealt with sin at the cross in order that a justifying God might deal with the sinner on the basis of atonement.

> On Jesus' cross this record's graved,
> Let sin be judged and sinners saved.

—Unknown

All Sin—Past, Present, and Future—Is Dealt With in the Cross

If you are a Christian and you have sinned, the Holy Spirit is convicting you. You must understand that all the fasting in the world will not take that sin away! All your promises and good deeds will not take that sin away. Reading the Bible will not take that sin away! Nothing but the blood of Jesus can remove sin!

And if all our sins are not atoned for in the death of Christ, then neither by confession nor prayer nor fasting nor any other means could they ever be forgiven.

Some are under the impression that Christ only bore some of their sins, those up to the time of conversion. They are troubled as to the question of their daily sins, as if these were to be disposed of upon a different ground from their past sins. They live as though Jesus died for all the sins they were guilty of before ever coming to know Him. But after that, they conclude, there must be some other way to deal with sin. But NO! Every sin is dealt with by the cross of Jesus and His shed blood!

Many can accept the pardon of God for those sins they are guilty of prior to conversion. With great faith, they can take hold of such great salvation and redemption by receiving the forgiveness of God.

However, after they are saved, it becomes difficult to believe that their sins can be forgiven. Satan uses their failures to build a stronghold, saying, "God can never bless you because of what you did as a Christian. God can never use you. Why do you think you are sick? You sinned; that's why you are sick! God is judging you for your sin."

These things come into our minds as arguments against the sure word of the testimony of Jesus Christ. The sure word of testimony is that He has not dealt with us according to our sins.

If you are walking in darkness as a believer and rejecting the counsel and correction of the Holy Spirit by refusing to obey what the Spirit is saying, then at that moment, you are rejecting His counsel. As a result, you choose agony! The only way back to fellowship is through the cross of Jesus.

As a believer, my communion may be interrupted, but my title can never be forfeited. Every trace of sin and guilt was atoned for by the sacrifice of Jesus.

God has been perfectly satisfied as to all believers' sins in the cross of Christ.

Our sins can never come into God's presence. He has laid everything on Christ, that the believer, at any moment of his life and any point in history, may say, "Thou hast cast all my sins behind thy back. Their sins and iniquities will I remember no more; He hath laid on Him the iniquities of us all." Christ, who bore all sin and put them away, now stands before God for me; it is no longer my sin that is before God.

"Likewise reckon ye also yourselves to be dead indeed unto sin, but alive unto God through Jesus Christ our Lord" (Romans 6:11). Such is the believer's unalterable position before God.

Gaining Peace Through the Blood of Jesus

Though God's justice is satisfied by the blood of Jesus and Satan's charges have been silenced, the one remaining demand has to be resolved. The believer must have peace in his spirit! If the believer fails to take by faith the work of the cross in regard to his sin, then very powerful strongholds can develop.

C.H. Mackintosh insists, though sin cannot affect God's thoughts in reference to us, it can—and does—affect our thoughts in reference to Him. Though sin cannot hide the Advocate from God's view, it can hide Him from ours.

You hear messages and read books, you memorize and confess Scripture, but there is a weight you carry because of the knowledge of your sins. You cannot pretend they don't exist. Telling yourself that God has forgiven you doesn't help, either. You need a reality of that forgiveness, and graciously God gives a practical way for obtaining it.

You must realize that though God loves you and has atoned for your sin, if you fall into sin, God will allow you to be upset by it. If we sin, our conscience will feel it. It must feel it! The Holy Ghost will make us feel it. He cannot allow so much as a single light thought to pass unjudged. What then? Has our sin made its way into the presence of God? God forbid! The Advocate—Jesus Christ the righteous— is there to maintain, in unbroken integrity, the relationship in which we stand.

The Bible says that if we confess our sins, He is faithful and just to forgive us our sins. The slightest unconfessed, unjudged sin on the conscience will entirely mar our communion with God. I know in my life, when I sin, I beg for forgiveness. I beg God to pardon me. I can go days begging. I want so much to know that I am forgiven. But I have to believe, according to the Scriptures, that when I confess to God, it is over; I am clean and restored in a moment! First, let me say that I believe in, and the Bible teaches, the need for asking for forgiveness. However, 1 John 1:9 does not say to ask for forgiveness, but to confess. So what is the difference?

Asking for forgiveness and pardon is part of confession. But it is not confession as a whole. If I am really confessing my sin, then I will ask for forgiveness. However, asking for forgiveness is easier than confessing. To simply say, "Please forgive me for doing wrong" is easier than being accountable for the full magnitude of my wrong. We know we have offended God, so we say, "Please forgive me." When asking for forgiveness, one may have in his mind things that tend to lessen the sense of the evil, secretly thinking that he was not so much to blame after all, though it is only proper to ask for forgiveness.

However, confession gives us more appreciation of His fellowship and how sin can take us from Him. So when I ask for forgiveness, I can be vague. But when I confess, I am bringing self-judgment upon myself, and I agree with God about the depth of my sinful activity. I agree that I am full of lust, or that I am a liar, or that I am greedy. I can blame no one else.

Some people ask for forgiveness just to be safe, never really understanding their offense. Their desire for forgiveness is not due to the loss of enjoying God's presence, but so they won't have to suffer eternal consequences.

A Christian, having erred in thought, word, or deed, might pray for pardon for days and months together and not have any assurance that he was forgiven, whereas the moment he truly confesses his sin before God, it is a simple matter of faith to know that he is perfectly forgiven and perfectly cleansed.

Were it possible for us, when we commit sin, to be forgiven merely for the asking, our sense of sin and our shrinking from it would not be so intense. As a consequence, our estimate of the fellowship with which we are blessed would not be as high.

It is utterly impossible that anyone can enjoy solid happiness until he is possessed of the divine assurance that the blood of the cross has canceled all his guilt. The devil can argue with me all he wants, but he cannot go to God with my sin. There he will be confronted by my Advocate and His blood!

In the atonement, we have remission and forgiveness of sins. In the richness of God's grace, He is able to forgive by the blood of Jesus. So will you let Him forgive you?

If you want a real answer to the sins of your past—those you find difficulty in being free of—then learn to confess. Openly and sincerely agree with God about what you are, not simply what you did.

Once again I conclude with a thought from C.H. Mackintosh, who says about the blood of Jesus:

Justice has owned it. The troubled conscience may rest in it. Satan must acknowledge it. Are you satisfied with Christ? Is He sufficient for thee? Art thou still searching for something in thyself, thy ways, thy works, thy thoughts, and thy feelings? If so, give up the search as utterly vain. Christ is sufficient for God; let Him be sufficient for thee.

The believer stands in grace, he is under grace, he breathes the very atmosphere of grace, and he never can be otherwise. If he commits sin, there must be confession. Then he will experience the forgiveness and cleansing of God on the ground of the faithfulness and justice of God. All is founded on the cross.

BREAKING THE STRONGHOLD OF REJECTION

CHAPTER 7

Rejection has a paralyzing effect, causing its victims to want to quit and give up. Their will is broken, and faith greatly damaged, all because somebody rejected them. Not only is rejection powerful in shutting a person down, but the fear of rejection has caused many never to act again, or even to live, for that matter. They are afraid of what might come. Haunted by the lies of rejection, they are afraid to move forward in life and take steps of faith because they choose to listen to rejection's voice: "What if they don't receive me? What if I speak of Christ at work and everybody rejects me for it? What if they hate me and want nothing to do with me? What if the Bible study doesn't go well?"

Everyone has experienced rejection. Everyone that God ever used greatly experienced rejection, but they went through it to the side of victory.

Rejection made *Elijah* want to die. It drove *Jehu* to the wilderness. It made the *psalmist* sorrowful as he lamented, "It wasn't an enemy but my own friend. Somebody I took sweet counsel with. We walked into the house of God together. We fellowshipped together. It was this one that rose up against me. Oh, that I had the wings of a dove to fly far away" (Psalm 55:6-14).

Moses was often rejected by Israel. They despised his leadership. His own family rejected his leadership. The *prophets* were killed. The *apostles* were martyred. Even *Jesus* was rejected by His own people. All of God's servants had to pass through the fire of rejection. *John Wesley* recorded in his writings:

May 5th a.m.: Preached in St. Ann's; was asked not to come back.

p.m.: Preached at St. John's; deacons said, "Get out and stay out."

May 12th a.m.: Preached at St. Jude's; can't go back there.

p.m.: Preached at St. George's; kicked out again.

May 19th a.m.: Preached at St. Andrew's; elders called special meeting and said not to return.

p.m.: Preached on the street and was run off.

May 26th a.m.: Preached in a field; got chased by a bull that was set loose.

June 2nd a.m.: Preached at the edge of town; police moved me.

I wonder how many of us at this point would have given up. Reasoning: I must not have heard God; I must not be called to be a preacher! Later, however, Wesley wrote:

p.m.: Preached in a pasture, and 10,000 people came!

If you want to see your life accomplish awesome things through the hands of God, you have got to be free from the stronghold of rejection. The natural tendency in man is to give up, to suffer from the fear of rejection. We think to ourselves, *No one likes me, no one wants to hear what I am saying, and everyone misunderstands me. It is just not working out, so I am going to quit.* Paul attacks this despair by saying, "Be ye steadfast, unmovable, always abounding in the work of the Lord" (1 Corinthians 15:58).

I have been there (wanting to quit and give up) many times in my life. Satan jumped on those moments of rejection and started reasoning with me, and my flesh was agreeing with him, that I should quit; I should give up. I have done all I can do. I have taken the people as far as I can take them; it must be over for me. I don't know how many times I have wrestled with that. But always, before God in prayer, there is an answer to that reasoning.

THE REJECTION OF JESUS

I think it is important to understand how rejection will affect us. Rejection means *to throw away, discard, or refuse as useless or unsatisfactory; refuse to accept.* This is bound to have an adverse effect upon our lives. It has to hurt.

The best example of how to handle rejection is Jesus. In His life we can see that it did affect him; it hurt and caused Him to weep. However, He was never brought into bondage over it. Experiencing the heartbreak of having someone reject you does not mean you are in a stronghold. Jesus did indeed experience rejection. However, He never suffered from the fear of being rejected. Jesus was without sin and failure in every area of His life.

Rejection Caused Jesus to Have Sorrow of Heart

Rejection is so powerful it can break your heart, "O Jerusalem, Jerusalem, *thou* that killest the prophets, and stonest them which are sent unto thee, how often would I have gathered thy children together, even as a hen gathereth her chickens under *her* wings, and ye would not" (Matthew 23:37).

Whenever anyone rejects you, you are going to suffer; your heart is going to be touched. Everyone wants to be liked. We want the approval of others. We can receive a thousand compliments then get one negative comment and forget about the compliments. All we can think about is that one rejection. We cannot seem to shake it. It has messed us up! We feel we are of no use anymore.

Many sports heroes say they have been driven by such passion. Though everyone in the world admires their ability and is willing to pay millions of dollars to see them perform, these grown men have broken down weeping like children over the rejection and lack of approval from their own fathers. They were unable to enjoy their success because of one man who refused to give them approval!

There is only one we must seek to please. We must have God's approval, which comes to us through the blood of Jesus Christ. We are not accepted of God by what we do, but by our faith in Jesus Christ. Now by this new birth, we can become vessels of honor for the Lord's glory. Our acceptance of God is through the blood of Jesus; our usefulness is the action of our faith.

Rejection Hindered Jesus' Immediate Plans

Jesus cried over Jerusalem, "How I have longed . . . but you would not." Because you rejected me, my desires for you have to be postponed.

Rejection, Brought About by Unbelief, Prevented Jesus From Showing People the Glory of God

> And when he was come into his own country, he taught them in their synagogue, insomuch that they were astonished, and said, Whence hath this *man* this wisdom, and *these* mighty works? Is not this the carpenter's son? is not his mother called Mary? and his brethren, James, and Joses, and Simon, and Judas? And his sisters, are they not all with us? Whence then hath this *man* all these things? And they were offended in him. But Jesus said unto them, A prophet is not without honour, save in his own country, and in his own house. And he did not many mighty works there because of their unbelief.
>
> Matthew 13:54-58

"He could do no miracles . . . ." They didn't reject Jesus because of His works and teachings. They rejected Jesus because of His past and His family. They could not get beyond His family. How could this Man be mighty? How could this Man be great? How could this Man be a prophet? He was brought up among us. There is His mother and brothers and sisters . . . . He is the Son of a carpenter! How can He be a miracle worker?

They rejected His future because of His past. Jesus was there to work miracles, to deliver the oppressed, to cast out devils, to heal the sick, to preach to the poor, and to lift up the brokenhearted. But this was family, His hometown. It was filled with cousins, aunts, uncles, brothers, and sisters. Therefore, they could not accept Him as the Son of God. They were not able to experience the power of God because of their unbelief. Many today suffer this same type of rejection because of those who will not believe that God is power-fully using their lives. If you are called by God to a life of ministry and power, then it is going to grieve your spirit to know how much people have missed out on God because they cannot accept who you are in Christ. Few things bring more grief to a preacher than for him to labor and pray, fast and hear God, and preach it to a people who will not receive it!

Rejection Prevented Jesus From Being Given the Honor He Deserved

People do not realize how transforming the power and anointing of God is upon a life that was once common. For thirty years, Jesus lived as a common man. He did not perform a miracle till He was about thirty years old. Prior to that, He just worked in the carpen-ter's shop. They watched Him grow up. They went to synagogue together. They played as children. They went to Jerusalem together. He is making chairs and tables; He is just like everyone else, so it seems!

But when He was baptized, and the Holy Ghost descended upon Him, everything changed. The anointing of God, the power of God, came upon Him. The manifestation and reality of everything God intended was going to be produced. He is the Messiah, He is the miracle worker, and He is the Lamb of God. Demons will be cast out. The lame will walk. The blind will see because this man is anointed of God. And still those who knew Him best dishonored Him by rejection.

So what did Jesus do? Did He quit and say that it was no longer worth it? No, He had to leave and get to the people who were looking for God and believing God. He refused to stay in a place where people were not listening and believing.

Bob Gass warns, "If you allow them to, the 'I knew you when' crew will keep you stuck at a stage in your life that's past and gone. You've got to move beyond the good old days! If you allow people

to keep taking you down memory lane, you'll eventually set up house, stay longer than you should, and miss your destiny."
Don't stay where you're tolerated; go where you're appreciated!

It's a gift to have people in your life who know where you've been and can relate to where you're going. But if you have to choose between *then* and *now*, sacrifice *then*. Keep in mind: It can't be rewritten, only replayed over and over again. Stop rehearsing your beginnings, and write the rest of your story!

If someone is rejecting you, you cannot live your life trying to get his approval. If everyone just says, "Well, that is just so and so. We knew him when he was a baby"—if that is all they can see because they don't recognize the power of God's anointing on your life, you will have to leave those people and that home and go where someone will be able to recognize the power of God upon your life.

THE REJECTION OF JOSEPH

> Joseph, *being* seventeen years old, was feeding the flock with his brethren . . . and Joseph brought unto his father their evil report. Now Israel loved Joseph more than all his children . . . and he made him a coat of *many* colours. And when his brethren saw that their father loved him more than all his brethren, they hated him, and could not speak peaceably unto him.
>
> Genesis 37:2 – 4

They hated Joseph. Perhaps Joseph made it easy for them to hate him. I would assume he had a clue they hated him because they were not kind to him. When he told them of his dreams and how they would honor him, this could have fueled their hatred. It is during this time that they seek to kill him. Instead, they decide to sell him as a slave. He ends up in Egypt. There he is falsely accused of a crime and thrown into prison. He is forgotten in prison. While in prison, the Pharaoh has a dream that no one can interpret. However, Joseph, the dreamer, is remembered and brought before Pharaoh. He interprets the dream and is immediately promoted to the position of prime minister.

As time passes, Joseph is given great authority in Egypt. While Joseph is enjoying prominence in Egypt, he is reunited with his brothers, and his dreams are fulfilled! The important thing to notice is Joseph's attitude and the strength of his faith:

> Now therefore be not grieved, nor angry with yourselves, that ye sold me hither: for God did send me before you to preserve life. (What an amazing statement. He explains that his brothers thought it was their actions but shows how it was God's hand that had sent him to Egypt.) For these two years *hath* the famine *been* in the land: and yet *there are* five years, in the which *there shall* neither *be* earing nor harvest. And God sent me before you to preserve you a posterity in the earth, and to save your lives by a great deliverance. So now *it was* not you *that* sent me hither, but God: and he hath made me a father to Pharaoh, and lord of all his house, and a ruler throughout all the land of Egypt. Haste ye, and go up to my father, and say unto him, Thus saith thy son Joseph, God hath made me lord of all Egypt: come down unto me, tarry not.
>
> Genesis 45:5-9

> And his brethren also went and fell down before his face; and they said, Behold, we *be* thy servants. And Joseph said unto them, Fear not: for *am* I in the place of God? (Joseph is saying that he is in the place God wants him to be.) But as for you, ye thought evil against me; *but* God meant it unto good, to bring to pass, as *it is* this day, to save much people alive.
>
> Genesis 50:18-20

From Jesus and Joseph, we can learn four ways to break the stronghold of rejection.

First, if someone has rejected you, you cannot spend the rest of your life trying to gain his acceptance.

Let him believe what he wants to believe and do what he wants to do, but you have to let it go. If he dies hating you, you cannot prevent that. You have to move on.

Second, be steadfast and unmovable in the calling of God upon your life.

We find from Joseph's testimony a very real truth regarding God that Paul would elaborate on even more. We know it in this simple phrase, "For we know that all things work together for good to those who love the Lord and are called according to His purpose."

Now, we understand that God promised Abraham the land of Canaan. However, the iniquity of the Canaanites was not at its peak. Therefore, God told him that his people would live in Egypt for about 400 years. After that, God would send a deliverer to bring them into the land of promise. In the mind of God, before Joseph was even a thought in the mind of Jacob, God had already anticipated how all these things were going to be fulfilled: Abraham is going to have a son, Isaac, who will have a son, Jacob. Jacob will have a son, Joseph, and his brothers are going to hate him. They will sell him into slavery. He is going into Egypt. He is going to be a slave in Potiphar's house. He is going to end up in prison. His integrity will be challenged, but I will sustain him. Then I will give Pharaoh a dream and tell Joseph what it means so he can deliver his people, and cause Abraham's seed to dwell in Egypt.

When Joseph was a seventeen-year-old boy describing these dreams to his family, they thought he was insane. However, Joseph always held on to this promise. He believed God, just as Jesus, for the joy that was set before Him, endured the cross. He saw and held on to the Father's will. He was a Man of sorrows, rejected of men and acquainted with grief. But He held on to the calling of God. He had the ability to pray on the cross, "Father, forgive them . . ." because He knew what He was doing. He knew where He was headed. He knew the plans of His Father. He was called by God, anointed by God; He was given the promise of God. He will give me the heathen as an inheritance! I will give my back to the smiters; I will give my life for that cause.

When it gets hard and there is the night of faith, when you don't know what God is doing, and it seems like everyone hates you and rejects you and no one wants to hear what you have to say—God has made you a promise! That is why John Wesley could be rejected day and night. They could turn the bulls loose on him, throw the stones at him, send him to jail, but he is going to be preaching in the morning. Why? There is a call on his life. God has sent him to do something. People can reject him and hate him, but there is something that God has called him to, and he refuses to let go of the promise!

Joseph had the promise and call of God, and it preserved him in that prison.

Do you know what he said to his brothers when he revealed himself to them? Here he is the prime minister of Egypt. He could have them executed. He said, "God has made me to forget." Now, he didn't forget the circumstances and all they did to him. He knew they hated him. What did he forget? He forgot the vengeance and desire to get them back. How could he do this? Because he realized, though his brothers meant to do him evil, this was the plan of God. It was a hard road. It was difficult. Joseph could have laid into them, arguing, "You don't know what it was like, seventeen years old, unable to see your father. You don't know what it is like to have all of your family hate you. You don't know what it is like to be a slave and be charged with crimes you never committed. But you also don't know what it is like to be prime minister! You don't know what it is like to walk by faith and hold on to the faithfulness of God! But the thing that kept me going was knowing that I am in the plan of God. He gave me a dream and told me that He would preserve my family. He told me He would bring me to a place of honor, and by God, He did it! And what you meant for evil, God meant for good; He has taken me through." This attitude is the same in everyone who has gotten past rejection.

If you don't know the calling of God on your life, the gifting of God for your life, and the anointing of God on your life, then you will suffer in that rejection. You must know why you are suffering. You must know who you are and why God has set you apart to this type of suffering.

You must make sure you keep your heart and life in a place where God can continue to use you. You cannot let your heart get bitter and filled with hatred and revenge. You must keep yourself in a place where God can continue to use you and speak to you. A person filled with bitterness and revenge will hinder the moving of God. Joseph, a man, shows us that it can be done in God.

Third, receive the courage God is going to give you.

You must believe that God has made you a promise. If thirteen years go by, which is about how much time passed for Joseph's sufferings, there might be some real battling as to whether you really heard God or not. You can try to hold on to the promise God has given you, but there comes a point when your faith must be tested. Do you really believe that you have a promise?

God is going to intervene and give you courage. He is the God of all comfort who comforts you in all your affliction.

I know that God gives courage. The problem is that we very seldom receive it. Most, instead of embracing what God is giving them, choose to play over and over again the rejection they have experienced. Numbers of people fail to receive God's courage. They give up; they cannot handle rejection, and their will to live is destroyed. However, courage from God can change everything. Just consider how God's courage helped and delivered these great men from fainting:

Joshua received courage from God after Moses died.

An angel was sent to Jesus in the garden.

Elijah was given Elisha.

Joseph was given a throne in Egypt.

Paul was given Epaphroditus.

Moses was given Jethro.

Wesley was given 10,000 people.

Jeremiah was given a fire in his bones! When he said he would quit, there was something of God in him that would not let him quit!

Is there something in you from heaven? Is it so strong that even if you were rejected by everyone, it would keep you going?

Fourth, no matter what I was, what my past was, what people think about me, I must know that the calling of God and the anointing of God break it all!

Oh, I knew Lee Shipp when . . . . But you need to know Lee Shipp now! What I was then and what I am now are different because of the calling of God on my life. By calling me, God has broken all the hindrances and limitations of my past. I can't let the voices of the past stop me. I must let the voice of the Holy Spirit lead me. If I allow rejection to stop me, I will not dream anymore; I will not hear God anymore. I will be too afraid to act.

BREAKING THE STRONGHOLD
OF CARNALITY

CHAPTER 8

W ithout controversy, the greatest weapon Satan has is the flesh, the carnality of man. The "flesh" is not the skin, but the nature that rules over man. 1 Corinthians 15 reveals that the first man is of the earth; he is earthy. Adam sought to satisfy his needs through the provisions that were in this world. He took of the fruit in the garden and pursued his own course against the commands of God. All the sons of Adam are doing that very thing today. We are following our father Adam. We are of the earth; therefore, we are earthy. We choose to allow this creation to be the means of our satisfaction.

The second man is of heaven; he is heavenly. This speaks of Christ. The nature of Christ did not seek satisfaction in the things of this world. By nature, He sought all satisfaction from the provisions of His Father's heavenly kingdom. Jesus was able to say that Satan comes and has nothing in Him.

Jesus' whole attitude was, "If I am satisfied, it will be by my Father's hand. When I am hungry, He will feed me. When I need counsel, He will give me wisdom. I will go to Him in prayer. I will go to Him with my needs. He will guide me. He will protect me. He will keep me from falling." This was the confidence Jesus had in His Father. But the first Adam and all of his sons, who say they are trusting God, put their confidence in their own ability and are driven by what they see, feel, and lust after.

Carnal simply refers to that which is of this world. It is not always "sinful," but it is limited and temporal. The alternative to carnal is spiritual. The spiritual man is Christ, and the carnal man is Adam.

Adam loves this world and the things that are in it (the worldly system: the mind, attitudes, and ways of the world). That worldly mind-set has no problem making its doctrine "Christian." Carnal men have a real problem because they allow the earth to be their source and satisfaction. Spiritual men are able to allow God and His entire kingdom to be their satisfaction.

Every problem in life comes when one chooses to be carnal rather than spiritual. There are many things the devil has access to in our carnal nature; there is a propensity in us to trust this world, to trust its logic. And by means of the world, Satan can cause all types of problems in our lives (depression, defeat, worry, etc). Only carnal men are worried about the economy. The spiritual man knows that he has never seen the righteous forsaken or his seed begging for bread, but it is the carnal man that thinks he has to do something to make it work out right.

Although the first man is of the earth and the second Man is the Lord from heaven, we must understand that both are men. Both are men in constitution, but one is earthy, and the other heavenly, which denotes the ruling nature in each.

Now, we don't want to take anything away from the humanity of Jesus Christ. When Jesus came into this world, He was fully man and fully God. He was tempted in every point as we are. That doesn't mean He was tempted with homosexuality, adultery, or stealing. The Bible says that all men are tempted in these points: the lusts of the flesh, the lusts of the eyes, and the pride of life. Jesus was tempted in all of these points, but He sinned not. He is the perfect and only sinless Man that God ever had.

How Carnality Shows Up in Man

Carnality shows up in man as the works of the flesh (Galatians 5). Adam was created in the image of God, but he took on the nature of sin (Genesis 5). This is the character of all Adam's sons and daughters. Galatians 5 reveals that if we do not crucify this flesh, we give

Satan an area where he can hinder us and set us back. The greatest avenue that Satan has into our lives is through our flesh.

The nature of carnality is also seen in the vanity of the Gentiles. Ephesians 4 says that we are not to walk as the Gentiles walk in the vanity of the mind. This command is given to the church so that we will not live like the Gentiles: in the vanity of the mind, doing things separated from God and living with a dark understanding. The carnal man does not know the will of God. He cannot understand why you are not worried about the things that worry him.

Romans 7 explains how the carnal nature shows up in the believer. He has the will power to do what is right, but he does not have the power in his will to perform accordingly. The will breaks down, and he is left without power. How hard he worked to do what was right! Finally, he discovers that victory through Christ is found by living in the Spirit.

Romans 8:5 reveals that death is working in us every time we try to do something apart from God. To be spiritually minded is life and peace because the spiritually minded only attempt things in the power of God. The carnal mind is at war with God. The carnal man has a struggle every time the offering plate is passed around. He knows theologically why people give, but he has a problem himself in giving. The carnal man comes into a worship service and allows his flesh to tell him he is too tired; therefore, he decides not to enter into the worship. The carnal wants to do the things of God but quickly comes to impossibility. The carnal cannot think the thoughts of God or perform the works of God. The carnal cannot even believe God. The carnal mind cannot cross the barrier of the natural and step into the supernatural. So where do you think the devil wants you?

The nature of carnality is also seen in those who worry and stress about life. In Matthew 6, Jesus is describing the basic needs of life: food, clothing, and shelter. He is not talking about lustful desires and immoral wants. He simply shows how the spiritual can live free of worry in regard to the basic needs of life. The Gentiles are seeking food, clothing, and shelter. Will this new job finally be the answer for me? Will this new investment be good for me? The carnal are seeking the things of the earth to maintain their comfortable lifestyle, with little confidence that God will provide.

Carnality also shows up as immaturity and limitation.

> And I, brethren, could not speak unto you as unto spiritual, but as unto carnal, *even* as unto babes in Christ. I have fed you with milk, and not with meat: for hitherto ye were not able *to bear it*, neither yet now are ye able. For ye are yet carnal: for whereas *there is* among you envying, and strife, and divisions, are ye not carnal, and walk as men?
>
> 1 Corinthians 3:1-3

Carnality shows up in the church as immaturity; the inability to understand the deep things of God. Carnal are those who must be satisfied with milk rather than meat. Divisions, strife, and schisms are all the effects of the carnal man acting in the church of God.

> We have many things to say, and hard to be uttered, seeing ye are dull of hearing. For when for the time ye ought to be teachers, ye have need that one teach you again which *be* the first principles of the oracles of God; and are become such as have need of milk, and not of strong meat. For every one that useth milk *is* unskilful in the word of righteousness: for he is a babe. But strong meat belongeth to them that are of full age, *even* those who by reason of use have their senses exercised to discern both good and evil.
>
> Hebrews 5:11-14

Carnal people in the church are dull of hearing; you can see it and feel it. They are physically there, but they are unable to participate and apply what God wants to do. They are listening, but they are not hearing; there is no expectation, no desire.

Carnality shows itself in the person who does not go on to maturity. It shows up among people who should be teachers and are not. Carnality shows up because men are not using their spiritual ability. They are not skillful in the Word of God or the ability to judge between good and evil.

James answers the question that so many would ask about the people of God: Why are they fighting and disputing one another?

From whence *come* wars and fightings among you? *Come they* not hence, *even* of your lusts that war in your members? Ye lust, and have not: ye kill, and desire to have, and cannot obtain: ye fight and war, yet ye have not, because ye ask not. Ye ask, and receive not, because ye ask amiss, that ye may consume *it* upon your lusts.

James 4:1-3

James said fights and disputes come from us. They do not come from Satan unless we let him in. If Satan gets in and is able to cause such damage, then he got in through someone's flesh. He told your flesh that it wasn't fair the way you were treated, and your flesh said, "You are right! It wasn't fair." He told your flesh, "They need to forgive you. They need to make apologies and come to you and seek your forgiveness. Until they do, you just need to distance yourself from them so that they will know that there is something they did that offended you and hurt you." And your flesh says, "That's right! They need to apologize." The carnal mind allows fighting and strife to come in.

The carnal nature in all of us has the potential to bring devastating problems in our walk with Christ and in the house of God. If a problem gets into the church and remains, it is because someone is determined to remain in the flesh. If the body of Christ (we as individuals) were determined to be spiritual, Satan would have no place to launch his attacks. The church would be mighty and triumphant. We would call that revival; we would know that God has visited His people!

The carnal mind cannot receive the things of the Spirit. The limitation is found in the lack of teachers. This results in inability to keep the body of Christ pure. Satan wants nothing more than to damage the reputation of Christ. There is no better way for him to do so than to cause sin and unhappiness among the people of God. After he has worked so hard to cause immorality, sin, and perversion in the church, Satan then takes the world and says, "Look what they did! They claimed to be Christians; they claimed to be redeemed, to be washed in the blood of the Lamb. They preach against this type of behavior! And look what they are doing."

There are people within the church who should be growing, maturing, and becoming skillful in the Word of God. They should become skillful to see when a brother is being overtaken and have the spiritual aptitude to deal with it so that it never goes so far as to hurt the testimony of Christ.

> It is reported commonly that there is fornication among you, and such fornication as is not so much as named among the Gentiles, that one should have his father's wife. And ye are puffed up, and have not rather mourned, that he that hath done this deed might be taken away from among you. For I verily, as absent in body, but present in spirit, have judged already, as though I were present, concerning him that hath so done this deed.
>
> 1 Corinthians 5:1-3

The shocking thing to Paul was not that there was sin in the church. The thing that upset the apostle most was how puffed up the Corinthians were! He is upset that they have not even wept about this. It has not disturbed them; the one who has done this deed has not been taken away from among them.

Paul is saying, "Do you want to know what a spiritual man would do about this? Do you want to know how God would want this handled? He would get that man out of the church. He would turn him over to Satan that his soul might be saved." That is a tough thing. Just try to excommunicate someone in this modern church era! Most of the church world will want to crucify the pastor for doing such a "heartless" thing.

But to the spiritual, there is one overriding passion: the reputation of Christ! It doesn't mean one is kicked out if he is found in sin. That would be an un-Christlike attitude toward those who are bound. First you go to them and discuss the issue. You go to help them, not to expose them. If they don't listen to you, then take some others with you. Then if they still refuse to listen, tell it to the church. If they don't listen to the church, then why should they be hanging out with the church? This is not done to be mean and "un-Christian." It is done to let them, and the world, know that this is not Christ!

Paul could not believe that the Corinthians were so puffed up about the way they handled this sinful behavior. They thought they were so spiritual, so holy, so close to God because they were able to take a person practicing incest and allow him to come and worship with them, saying, "We can accept him in the love of God." That floored Paul! "I speak to your shame. Is it so, that there is not a wise man among you? no, not one that shall be able to judge between his brethren?" (1 Corinthians 6:5).

Summing Up

The carnality of man is summed up in this fashion—**UNBELIEF!** Fundamentally, the carnal man cannot rest on the Word of God. He does not forgive because of unbelief! He does not mature because of unbelief! He is not filled because of unbelief!

Because he cannot believe God, he seeks worldly provisions. In religion, he seeks to understand naturally and fulfill in his will power what can only be done spiritually!

He knows the Lord says to be spiritual, to seek His kingdom and righteousness, but he continues on from day to day with the same worries and pursuits that the Gentiles have. Belief is not saying, "Amen," and nodding in agreement. Belief is the passion to live by faith what God has made known to me!

The Mighty Weapon of God

> Whereby are given unto us exceeding great and precious promises: that by these ye might be partakers of the divine nature, having escaped the corruption that is in the world through lust.
>
> 2 Peter 1:4

Through these promises, we can escape the corruption that is in the world. Why is it that some will not take God at His word? Because of their unbelief. I believe there is an answer to this carnal self. There is an answer to the frustration of this flesh. God gives me the Holy Ghost so that I do not have to live in "myself" anymore. He can put the mind of Christ in me because the mind of Lee Shipp is never going to agree with God. My mind may agree that God said it. It sounds good, but I just cannot do it!

I cannot do what God said to do. I cannot walk on water. I cannot speak to the sun and have it stop. I cannot go and pray over somebody who is blind so he might see. But the mind of Christ can! The mind of Jesus will walk on water. He will speak to the sun and pray for the blind to see. He will face every Goliath and cross every river, and while He is doing so, he will proclaim, "Sirs, I believe God!"

I am praying for the sick because I believe God.

I am stepping out in faith because I believe God.

I am not seeking this world and all of its temptations because I believe God.

I choose to forgive because I believe God.

I am letting go of bitterness and my past because I believe God.

I am living free and will not be depressed anymore because I believe God.

Faith receives the grace to labor to the very end so it can be free. I am not saying that your carnality is forever removed. You will wrestle with your flesh until Jesus comes, but the answer to carnality is to believe God for the provisions to overcome this sin nature. That provision is the Holy Ghost and the mind of Christ.

The spiritual man is not a perfected man who never fights his flesh. He simply is able to realize and recognize a lack of progress in Christ. He is able to admit, "I am not praying like I should. I am not studying the Bible like I should."

The carnal man will set his alarm clock thirty minutes early. He is going to do everything he can, through will power, to get up to pray and study because that is what he thinks he should do.

The spiritual mind will get to an altar! He will cry out to God, "I need your Spirit! If your Spirit will come on me, You will wake me up in the morning. You will cause me to pray without ceasing."

The carnal mind knows things are not right with God, and he is going to do something about it. The spiritual man knows he is not right with God and must do something about it at an altar.

The spiritual man knows when his heart is getting filled with lust. He recognizes that he is lusting after the things in this world. He understands there is bitterness in his heart. He knows the answer to the lust and bitterness is not in trying to stop it, but in confessing it: "God, I need Your help. I can't do anything but this. Please fill me with the Holy Ghost that I may be free again." He goes after God like Elisha went after Elijah.

Faith Is the Substance of the Spiritual Life

Simply put, without faith in God, what good are the promises He makes us. Without faith, it is impossible to please Him. Without faith, you are but a man among men. You have forsaken the supernatural for the natural. If by faith you would receive these precious promises, you would become a terror to hell and a bulwark of heaven!

The stronghold of carnality must be shattered. I MUST BELIEVE GOD! I MUST BE SPIRITUAL, even when every voice and logic is against me:

"How can you tithe when things are so tight?"

"That I may boldly say, 'The Lord is my helper!'"

"How can you move on in such pain and shattered dreams?"

"Because the Lord has promised good to me!"

I must want God to satisfy me and seek His provision only.

Satan Is Defeated When the Stronghold of Carnality Is Broken!

When do you think Goliath was defeated? Goliath was not defeated by the rock.

All Israel trembled before Goliath because they were carnal! But God had an answer to their carnality. If Goliath was ever to be defeated and shut up, the answer was not another giant of a man; I must get a spiritual man in there. Here he comes with the cart of cheese!

Goliath was defeated when David killed the bear and wolf and had the revelation, "He taught my hands to war!" It was when he pulled off Saul's armor and put on the promises of God and said, "Goliath, you come at me in carnality (with sword and spear), but I come to you in the NAME OF THE LORD!

Living here is freedom, contentment, victory, rest, and joy!

BREAKING THE STRONGHOLD
OF PAIN

CHAPTER 9

"Men groan from out of the city, and the soul of the wounded crieth out: yet God layeth not folly *to them*" (Job 24:12). Slip into this scene . . . a busy metropolis . . . speed . . . movement . . . noise. The activity of a typical city: shoppers . . . store owners unlocking the doors for business . . . cars . . . traffic . . . the fresh smells of the bakeries . . . the laughter of children. You can see it; you can smell the scene. But there is more. Behind and beneath the loud splash of human activity are invisible aches, not from an alley where a drifter may be suffering something physical. No, these groans are coming from the souls of those walking the street or pulling into the bakery for some fresh bread.

Job says these groans come from one who has been wounded: "The souls of the wounded cry out." Job says the soul is wounded. The soul is crying out, perhaps from a broken heart, offenses that have been brought against that life. It is a painful wound. The Bible says these groans arise from the city. Buried somewhere . . . unnoticed . . . uncared for are the groans of the wounded; their hearts have deep lacerations. The scars are so deep, the wounds so painful that it is the soul of the man that is crying. The pain and wounds are so severe that there is no surgeon on earth who can bring healing or relief. "The spirit of a man will sustain his infirmity; but a wounded spirit who can bear?" (Proverbs 18:14).

What are the wounded to do? God reveals Himself as One who greatly desires to deliver and heal the wounded spirit!

The LORD . . . gathereth together the outcasts . . . . He healeth the broken in heart, and bindeth up their wounds.

Psalm 147:2-3

Hast thou not known? hast thou not heard, that the everlasting God, the LORD, the Creator of the ends of the earth, fainteth not, neither is weary? There is no searching of his understanding. He giveth power to the faint; and to them that have no might he increaseth strength . . . they that wait upon the LORD shall renew their strength; they shall mount up with wings as eagles; they shall run, and not be weary; and they shall walk, and not faint.

Isaiah 40:28-29

For thus saith the high and lofty One that inhabiteth eternity, whose name *is* Holy; I dwell in the high and holy *place*, with him also *that is* of a contrite and humble spirit, to revive the spirit of the humble, and to revive the heart of the contrite ones.

Isaiah 57:15

The high and lofty One, the God who inhabits eternity, says, "Do you know who dwells with me? Do you know who has my presence? It is the contrite and humble in spirit." God revives the spirit of the contrite and humble, and brings down the haughty and proud. Those who enjoy God's presence are not the ones who feel it is deserved. God will reject the approach of the haughty. Those who are broken are allowed before His throne, and He lifts them up.

What a picture of God. See His might, how high and lifted up He is, and how He gently takes the broken and humble in His mighty hands, picks them up, lifts them and holds them close to Himself.

I will seek that which was lost, and bring again that which was driven away, and will bind up *that which was* broken, and will strengthen that which was sick: but I will destroy the fat and the strong; I will feed them with judgment.

Ezekiel 34:16

God will bring back that which was lost. He will make strong those who were sick. He will bind up those who were broken. And all who consider themselves strong and have no real need for God, He will break.

A portion of 2 Corinthians deals with a particular judgment brought against a young sinner. The sin was so bad he had to be excommunicated from the church. Through this discipline, he fell under conviction and repented, coming back to God. Paul then instructed the church at Corinth to receive him back, forgive him: "So that contrariwise ye *ought* rather to forgive *him*, and comfort *him*, lest perhaps such a one should be swallowed up with overmuch sorrow!" (2 Corinthians 2:7).

He has gone through a very difficult time. Comfort him lest the sorrow he has been experiencing overwhelms him, and as a result, he may never find deliverance! Church, your ministry is important to those who are under conviction. So that the sorrow ends and the joyful restoration can begin, you must offer the repentant fellowship and comfort in the name of Christ. The restoration and healing of His people is always the desire of God. It is wonderful that the almighty God does not want to destroy us. It is good to know that He wants to heal us and deliver us.

> Wherefore lift up the hands which hang down, and the feeble knees; And make straight paths for your feet, lest that which is lame be turned out of the way; but let it rather be healed.
>
> Hebrews 12:12-13

The discipline of God is grievous for all upon whom this correction must fall. However, the Bible says to lift up our hands and make feeble knees strong and walk straight. If we walk with murmuring and complaining and overbearing sorrow and guilt, then we may cause others who are weak and lame to stumble away. Instead, we should rejoice in a fatherly God who loves us so much that He is willing to correct us. We need to rejoice in a God who has so much power that He is able to take our brokenness and make it strong; He is able to take feeble people and do wonderful things through them. He is able to take Christians who sin, wash them in the blood of Jesus, and make them holy! We rejoice that He disciplines us and perfects those things that concern us. Oh, thank You, God, that You love me. Thank You for keeping those thoughts out of my mind. Thank You for not letting me get away with my sin. Before I was saved, I never felt conviction about any of these things. Thank You for demanding my holiness!

Then when the young and weak see us being disciplined with such thankfulness and rejoicing, they understand that the way of God's children in times of reproof is the way of joy and thankfulness!

In the city are the groans of men. Even within the church are the groans of men. We don't always hear it, but in every service, people are groaning, and their hearts have been wounded. Their reputations are being attacked. They have enemies against their lives. Somebody has hurt them. Somebody has slandered them. Somebody has assaulted them.

Right now there is someone who hears your groan. Jesus hears your groan. He sees your heart. And what no surgeon on earth can heal, He confidently says, "The Spirit of the Lord *is* upon me, because he hath anointed me to preach the gospel to the poor; he hath sent me to heal the brokenhearted, to preach deliverance to the captives, and recovering of sight to the blind, to set at liberty them that are bruised" (Luke 4:18).

If you are hurting, if you have been molested, if your spirit is dying, the physician has come to heal you, to make you whole! If you can humble yourself, have a contrite spirit, and be honest with God about your life, if you can say, "Yes, God, I am hurting; I have been broken; I am unhappy; I am not right," then I have good news. God anointed Jesus to bring you deliverance. The Father heard your groan, and He sent Jesus to heal you.

We Must Be Healed

What I am driving at is the fact that we must be healed. Wounded spirits must become well! Yes, there is hurting and pain, but there is a God who heals. He is not glorified in our sickness or groaning, but in our rejoicing. We must be free from a wounded spirit; nobody can bear the wounded spirit very long! Regardless of how the pain and groaning comes, God is working it for the purpose of circumcising our hearts. "And circumcision is that of the heart, in the spirit, and not in the letter . . ." (Romans 2:29).

This circumcision is to tear our heart and rip it to the spiritual nature of our lives. It is to bring our soul to a place of desperate pain. When we come into this new life with Jesus, our hearts are being changed. There is the forsaking of old friendships, the giving up of old habits, and the crucifying of our flesh. Today we are so desperate to preserve our hearts from being hurt, we want to avoid the pain of circumcision. But God is committed to the circumcision of our hearts: He will break it, tear it, and separate it.

Many Christians have experienced some of the tearing of the heart, the wounding of the heart. It is a very painful experience. Sadly, this is as far as many Christians have gotten. They have gone as far as the wounding of the heart and never experienced the place of healing. And many hold secret bitterness in their heart to God, "Look at all I have given up for You, God. Look at the things I have suffered for You. And this is all I get out of it—this heartache, this pain? It seems the advantages of Christianity never come my way. I look at other Christians, and they seem so blessed, so happy, so prosperous. But all I have is misery, pain."

The reason is that you never allowed the wound to heal! You never allowed the heart to become whole! Circumcision is the pain that naturally occurs, but healing is the result that God is after. It is not until we are healed that God will allow us to enjoy the freedom of a life without reproach. Just consider God's instructions to Joshua.

When Israel Was Free

And it came to pass, when they had done circumcising all the people, that they abode in their places in the camp, till they were whole. And the LORD said unto Joshua, This day have I rolled away the reproach of Egypt from off you. Wherefore the name of the place is called Gilgal unto this day.

Joshua 5:8-9

God demanded circumcision from the children of Israel, and He told them to remain in that place until they were healed. There was a definite wound, and there would be a definite healing. So many believers think their reproach is removed with the circumcision. But God said that it would not be till they were healed—THEN . . .

THAT DAY.

GOD—not you . . .

God ROLLED away . . .

God rolled away the REPROACH . . .

God rolled away reproach from YOU!

Don't Do Anything Until You Are Healed

Until the healing came, they were not to do anything. God said that when you are healed, He will remove your reproach. You will not have the mentality of slaves anymore. You will not be beaten down anymore. You will take every city. You will overcome every giant. You will receive every promise. All nations of the earth will know that the Lord is your God!

But God's people had to be healed for that to happen. As long as they were wounded from the circumcision, a group of children could have invaded their tribe and killed the whole of them because the men were in such pain. And that is what happens to many believers. They get hurt, and then the slightest things seem to overcome them. They are so easily offended, so quickly distraught! Instead of healing, they pick at the wound. They relive the pain over and again. Or they keep fooling around with the world; they keep fooling around with old friends and habits, never allowing themselves to heal. And eventually, they decide not to be close to people anymore, or their fellowship in the church diminishes, and they are no longer in the prayer meeting. Sadly, they leave the place where they can be healed, and they never get over their wounds.

When you have been circumcised in your heart, you must wait until you are healed. God then removes the reproach of this world from your life. No longer are you a servant of this world! You are not a slave to the devil anymore. You will receive his promises. You are able to give thanks in all things and rejoice always! Every obstacle is a stepping stone for a heart that has been healed. You will walk in places you never dreamed you would.

God Is After a Healed Heart

God is after the joy of a free and healed heart! This heart that has been afflicted by God, circumcised, and healed by God is a heart that is free of every stronghold hell would try to put in that life.

A healed heart is found in Psalm 51.

> Behold, thou desirest truth in the inward parts: and in the hidden part thou shalt make me to know wisdom. Purge me with hyssop, and I shall be clean: wash me, and I shall be whiter than snow. Make me to hear joy and gladness; that the bones which thou hast broken may rejoice. Hide thy face from my sins, and blot out all mine iniquities. Create in me a clean heart, O God; and renew a right spirit within me. Cast me not away from thy presence; and take not thy holy spirit from me. Restore unto me the joy of thy salvation; and uphold me with thy free spirit.
>
> Psalm 51:6-12

The healed don't hide anymore. They have trusted God with their hearts.

People who are wounded in spirit are so hard to bear. You love them, but they just cannot be helped. They are depressed and cynical and refuse any solution.

However, how wonderful are the healed; they are able to say things like:

> No matter where I am blown or pushed,
> I will flourish!
> Those with less strength would wilt and die
> On the soil on which I now stand.
> But because I DO love the Lord,
> I WILL SURVIVE AND IMPROVE!
> Others might expect me to wither,
> But God expects me to bloom.

97

I will show them how tough I am—
I will bloom—IN AND OUT OF SEASON.

—Source unknown

There is no permanent calamity
For any child of God;
Way stations all, at which we briefly stop
Upon our homeward road.
Our pain and grief are only travel stains
Which shall be wiped away,
Within the blessed warmth and light of home,
By God's own hand some day.

—Martha Snell Nicholson[1]

Choose to love—rather than hate
Choose to smile—rather than frown
Choose to build—rather than destroy
Choose to persevere—rather than quit
Choose to praise—rather than gossip
Choose to heal—rather than wound
Choose to give—rather than grasp
Choose to act—rather than delay
Choose to forgive—rather than curse
Choose to pray—rather than despair.

DON'T FORGET
Life is about 10 percent how you make it . . .
And 90 percent how you take it.

- Unkown

Sometimes I Think
I Understand Everything
Then I Regain Consciousness

—Ashleigh Brilliant[2]

"I can do all things through Christ who strengtheneth me."

—Paul

Two brothers who lived on adjoining farms fell into conflict. It was the first serious rift in forty years of farming side by side, sharing machinery and trading labor and goods as needed.

It all fell apart by a small misunderstanding, and it grew into a major difference. Then it finally exploded into bitterness.

One morning there was a knock on John's door. He opened it to find a Man with a carpenter's toolbox. "I'm looking for a few days' work. Perhaps you would have a few small jobs here and there I could help with?"

"Yes," said John. "I do have a job."

"Look across the creek at that farm. That's my neighbor; in fact, it's my younger brother. Last week there was a meadow between us, and he took his bulldozer to the river levee, and now there is a creek between us. He might have done this to spite me, but I'll go him one better. See that pile of lumber? I want you to build me a fence so I won't need to see his place or his face anymore."

The Carpenter said, "I think I understand the situation. Show me the nails and the materials, and I'll be able to do a job that pleases you."

John went to town, and the Carpenter worked hard all day, measuring, sawing, nailing. When John returned, the Carpenter had just finished the job.

The farmer's eyes opened wide; his jaw dropped. There was no fence there at all. It was a bridge—a bridge stretching from one side of the creek to the other! A fine piece of work, handrails and all—and the younger brother was coming across, his hand outstretched, saying, "You are quite a man to build this bridge after all I've said."

The two brothers stood at each end of the bridge, and then they met in the middle, taking each other's hand.

The Carpenter was on His way off when they asked Him to stay. He said, "I'd love to stay on, but I have many more bridges to build."

BREAKING THE STRONGHOLD
OF PRIDE

CHAPTER 10

Pride must be the greatest of strongholds. Nothing hinders the working of God more than pride. Unbelief, carnality, and self-ishness are horrible sins, but the thing that keeps people from being delivered from carnality, unbelief, and selfishness is pride! Pride is a horrible wickedness.

God Cannot Suffer the Proud

Notice the attitude of God toward those who are prideful:

Him that hath an high look and a proud heart will not I suffer.

Psalm 101:5

The Bible says that God will not suffer the proud. God does not say this about adulterers, murderers, or drunkards. God says this to the proud! The word "suffer" has to do with patience. God is saying that He will not tolerate, He will not endure the proud. He deals with them severely. God has great patience toward those who are strug-gling with sin. But when someone has rested in his sinful pride, God will not tolerate him. He will bring him down!

Though the LORD be high, yet hath he respect unto the lowly: but the proud he knoweth afar off.

Psalm 138:6

God will not let the proud near Him; He keeps them at a distance. Notice what Jesus said:

> Two men went up into the temple to pray; the one a Pharisee, and the other a publican. The Pharisee stood and prayed thus with himself, God, I thank thee, that I am not as other men *are*, extortioners, unjust, adulterers, or even as this publican. I fast twice in the week, I give tithes of all that I possess. And the publican, standing afar off, would not lift up so much as *his* eyes unto heaven, but smote upon his breast, saying, God be merciful to me a sinner. I tell you, this man went down to his house justified *rather* than the other: for every one that exalteth himself shall be abased; and he that humbleth himself shall be exalted.
>
> Luke 18:10-14

How often do we find ourselves in the place of the Pharisee? As the Pharisee, our perceived worth before God is based upon our noble religious accomplishments: We resisted sin, we went above our tithes and gave great offerings, or we spent the week in such great fasting and prayer. So we approach the presence of God with our performance. There is such arrogance in approaching God this way. Our only right before the presence of God is the work and merit of Jesus and His blood. A person with a prideful heart cannot be near God!

> These six things doth the LORD hate: yea, seven are an abomination unto him: A proud look, a lying tongue, and hands that shed innocent blood.
>
> Proverbs 6:16-17

The first thing on God's list is pride!

> The fear of the LORD is to hate evil: pride, and arrogancy, and the evil way, and the froward mouth, do I hate.
>
> Proverbs 8:13

Here Solomon is describing evil. Evil is composed of pride, arrogance, and the evil way.

> Every one that is proud in heart is an abomination to the LORD: though hand join in hand, he shall not be unpunished.

Proverbs 16:5

God is going to punish the proud, even if every one of them are joined together to defy God. God aggressively opposes the proud, and He will humble them, not necessarily convert them! He wants to convert them, but if they refuse, then He will humble them. Though there is a season of His grace, He cannot tolerate or endure the proud spirit.

So What Exactly Is Pride?

The essence of pride is a fool. According to Scripture, a fool is someone who does not fear God. The fool demonstrates contempt for God by acting in the place of God!

Pride is something within a man, causing him to take action that only God should take. It causes the man to pursue results that only God can produce; he thinks as though in his own puny self, he can accomplish what only God can! The prideful fool has disregard for God in the heart. He reasons within himself, "If it is ever to be done, I must do it!" And he takes matters into his own hands.

God opposes pride to such length that He cast Satan out of heaven. And man has always sought what Satan wanted! Man has joined with Satan to enthrone himself above God. Man has always wanted to be God; he has passionately pursued it.

Every kind of sin can be cleansed and forgiven, even pride! But we must realize that pride has a devilish quality that hinders a person from taking responsibility. Pride causes one to stubbornly refuse to humble himself and confess his fault to God. It doesn't mean he doesn't know what to do; however, pride is that which keeps him from doing it! It is rare for proud hearts to heed correction.

My prayer has always been, "God, never let me become so full of pride that I lose my ability to repent!" No one is more difficult to deal with than a prideful person.

God told me that He would send people into my life to keep me humble, whether it was a friend or an enemy, a theologian or a child. Sometimes I will be offended; other times hurt, and when that comes, I need to keep humble. And I am telling you that I have fought my prideful heart. Every time someone has brought reproof into my life, I can feel the pride rising up in me! I can feel the need for self-justification soaring up in me. How I want to put that person in his place and establish myself as someone higher and greater and somehow untouchable!

I don't want to be so calloused about anything, even if it is small and insignificant. Only pride would make me feel any sin is small.

Conviction of sin is one of the rarest things that ever strikes a man. It is the threshold of an understanding of God. Jesus Christ said that when the Holy Spirit rouses a man's conscience and brings him into the presence of God, it is not his relationship with men that bothers him, but his relationship with God—"against Thee, Thee only, have I sinned, and done this evil in Thy sight." The marvels of conviction of sin, forgiveness, and holiness are so interwoven that it is only the forgiven man who is the holy man, he proves he is forgiven by being the opposite to what he was, by God's grace. Repentance always brings a man to this point: I have sinned. The surest sign that God is at work is when a man says that and means it. Anything less than this is remorse for having made blunders, the reflex action of disgust at himself.

The entrance into the Kingdom is through the panging pains of repentance crashing into a man's respectable goodness; then the Holy Ghost, Who produces these agonies, begins the formation of the Son of God in the life. The new life will manifest itself in conscious repentance and unconscious holiness, never the other way about. The bedrock of Christianity is repentance. Strictly speaking, a man cannot repent when he chooses; repentance is a gift of God. The old Puritans used to pray for the "gift of tears." If ever you cease to know the virtue of repentance, you are in darkness. Examine yourself and see if you have forgotten how to be sorry.

—Oswald Chambers

It seems that Solomon spent a lot of time studying the proud, and in Proverbs, he describes many of their character traits.

Solomon said that the proud refuse correction; therefore, they refuse to repent! Proverbs 10:17 reads:

He is in the way of life that keepeth instruction: but he that refuseth reproof erreth.

Because he is proud, Solomon said that he rejects counsel. Proverbs 12:15 reads:

The way of a fool is right in his own eyes: but he that hearkeneth unto counsel is wise.

The proud will even shun the helpful insight of a father's instruction. Proverbs 15:5 reads:

A fool despiseth his father's instruction: but he that regardeth reproof is prudent.

Solomon said that a proud man will go to his grave before he will listen to a wise man's advice. Proverbs 15:10, 12 reads:

Correction is grievous unto him that forsaketh the way: and he that hateth reproof shall die. A scorner loveth not one that reproveth him: neither will he go unto the wise.

Because the proud are blind, they endanger their soul by their arrogance before God. Proverbs 15:32-33 reads:

He that refuseth instruction despiseth his own soul: but he that heareth reproof getteth understanding. The fear of the LORD is the instruction of wisdom; and before honour is humility.

Solomon said that the proud are worse than fools because a fool has a chance of seeing his foolishness. However, the proud are blind, even when everyone around them can see how foolish they are. Proverbs 26:12 reads:

Seest thou a man wise in his own conceit? there is more hope of a fool than of him.

Jeremiah said that the proud will greatly damage the heart of those who love them the most. Jeremiah 13:16-17 reads:

Give glory to the LORD your God, before he cause darkness, and before your feet stumble upon the dark mountains, and, while ye look for light, he turn it into the shadow of death, and make it gross darkness. But if ye will not hear it, my soul shall weep in secret places for your pride; and mine eye shall weep sore, and run down with tears, because the LORD's flock is carried away captive.

And finally, Solomon said that the proud are to be avoided. You had sooner meet an angry bear than a fool in his pride. Proverbs 17:12 reads:

Let a bear robbed of her whelps meet a man, rather than a fool in his folly.

This is the condition, and the awful results, of the proud.

So What Hope Do the Proud Have?

If they are so arrogant, what ever do we say to them? We must tell them the truth, counsel them to abandon their pride and selfish wisdom, tell them to become a fool that they may be wise.

Let no man deceive himself. If any man among you seemeth to be wise in this world, let him become a fool, that he may be wise. For the wisdom of this world is foolishness with God. For it is written, He taketh the wise in their own craftiness.

1 Corinthians 3:18-19

Speak the truth to the proud, and trust the Holy Spirit to reach them. Tell them something like this: "If you think you are so smart that you have it all figured out, then abandon that thought! Realize that is the most absurd thing a human can think. Become a fool. Come to a place where you have no answers, no explanations. Come to a place where you cannot explain why you did what you did. Admit that you cannot explain why things happen the way they happen. Then humbly and fearfully bow down before the fact that there is a God who knows all! Get to the place where you have to trust God."

People keep themselves from Christ because they say they are intellectuals. But these are not intellectuals; the Bible calls them fools! God says quit deceiving yourself. Do you really think it is your intellect that is keeping you from God? Do you really think it is because you are so wise that you cannot be converted? Quit deceiving yourself!

Three Areas Where Proud People Parade Their Arrogance

First, they play God when they determine what's best for their lives. I can see this form of pride in my prayers. I see it in my writings. I hear it in my thoughts. I feel it and hear it in my heart when I entertain silent reasonings such as, "But God, I did this for You . . . . God, I deserve this . . . . God, this should not have happened . . . . God, why me? . . . . God, it is not fair!" I act as though God is not doing anything in my life, and He has totally forsaken and abandoned me.

God showed me that is nothing but pride! God told me something along this line: "Because you are putting yourself in My place, and you think you know what is best for your life, and you think you could do a better job than I, you are playing God. When you think you know what would help you more than I do, you are full of pride. I told you in My Word that I am working everything out together for your good. If you would trust Me and have faith in Me, you would see everything that I am bringing to pass!"

God shall likewise destroy thee for ever, he shall take thee away, and pluck thee out of thy dwelling place, and root thee out of the land of the living. Selah (now pause and consider who God will do this to). Lo, this is the man that made not God his strength; but trusted in the abundance of his riches, and strengthened himself in his wickedness

Psalm 52:7

Remember what wickedness is. It is pride! It is the effort to build myself up by thinking I can do it better with the resources at my disposal. It is the type of reasoning that suggests that if my children are going to be saved, then I have to do something. It is pride when my heart says, "I have asked the Holy Spirit to save them, and nothing has happened; I have to do something!"

God warned Israel of this dangerous attitude:

And thou say in thine heart, My power and the might of mine hand hath gotten me this wealth. But thou shalt remember the LORD thy God: for it is he that giveth thee power to get wealth, that he may establish his covenant which he sware unto thy fathers, as it is this day.

Deuteronomy 8:17-18

When I consider these Scriptures and what it means to play God in my life (what I consider unfair, what I think I should have, things I think I deserve, what I think God ought to be doing for me), then I quickly come to this realization that I should never cast a frown upon the throne of God. When I begin to question the painful experiences in my life, as though I deserve better, I should abandon my pride and be grateful that God has not dealt with me according to my sins. I should be thankful that He is not sitting up in heaven making sure there is justice in everything that concerns me. Because if God just measured out justice, I know what I deserve, and it is not blessings!

It is my pride that refuses to see His compassions and mercy upon me! When I begin to reason within myself by such things as, "If I were God, I would . . .," then I must repent. I cannot weasel out of this. I have to accept the reproof that the Holy Spirit is giving me and say, "God, You are right! I am prideful. I am not thankful. I do think I could do better sometimes. I think I deserve better when You have been so good to me—blessing me and my family."

Second, the proud play God by controlling people. The proud manipulate others to do what they want them to do. The proud call it looking out for the interest of others and acting for their own good. But a lot of times, it is nothing more than an attempt to play God.

The proud coerce people to feel obligated to see things the way they see them and to feel the way they feel. So the proud connive, manipulate, and work to bring people to their arrogant position. Even if their position is right, it must not be their power that brings others to that position; it can only be God! "And my speech and my preaching was not with enticing words of man's wisdom, but in demonstration of the Spirit and of power: That your faith should not stand in the wisdom of men, but in the power of God" (1 Corinthians 2:4-5).

Four friends came to comfort Job in his calamity. These four were in contention with one another. Now, what these men said was correct; you could preach sermons on their theology. The problem was their application of truth, so God considered them to be foolish.

> Should not the multitude of words be answered? and should a man full of talk be justified? Should thy lies make men hold their peace? and when thou mockest, shall no man make thee ashamed?
>
> Job 11:2-3

Job's friends were convinced that Job's suffering was the result of personal sin.

For thou hast said, My doctrine *is* pure, and I am clean in thine eyes. But oh that God would speak, and open his lips against thee; And that he would show thee the secrets of wisdom, that *they are* double to that which is! Know therefore that God exacteth of thee *less* than thine iniquity *deserveth.*

Job 11:4-6

Zophar continues to beg Job for his repentance:

If iniquity *be* in thine hand, put it far away, and let not wickedness dwell in thy tabernacles. For then shalt thou lift up thy face without spot; yea, thou shalt be stedfast, and shalt not fear . . .

Job 11:14-15

In sarcasm Job said,

No doubt but ye *are* the people, and wisdom shall die with you.

Job 12:1-2

Did you ever have somebody like this in your life? He thought he had it all figured out and knew exactly why you were suffering, yet he was so far from the truth?
Eliphaz said,

Should a wise man utter vain knowledge, and fill his belly with the east wind? Should he reason with unprofitable talk? or with speeches wherewith he can do no good? Yea, thou castest off fear, and restrainest prayer before God. For thy mouth uttereth thine iniquity, and thou choosest the tongue of the crafty. Thine own mouth condemneth thee, and not I: yea, thine own lips testify against thee. *Art* thou the first man *that* was born? or wast thou made before the hills? Hast thou heard the secret of God? and dost thou restrain wisdom to thyself? What knowest thou, that we know not?

what understandest thou, which *is* not in us? With us *are* both the grayheaded and very aged men, much elder than thy father (not only are we older than you, Job, we are older than your father; we know, we have been around!).

Job 15:2-10

Can you see where the pride is and how it is being used? They are determined to make Job see things the way they see things.
Bildad said,

How long *will it be ere* ye make an end of words? mark, and afterwards we will speak. Wherefore are we counted as beasts, *and* reputed vile in your sight?

Job 18:2-3

Bildad wants to know when Job is going to be quiet so he can finally listen to what he and his peers have to say. When is Job finally going to be quiet and listen to their wisdom? Why are you so upset with us, Job? Why do you treat us as beasts? Don't you know that we love you and have come to help you? We want to help you and pull you out of your sin.
Job says,

Yea, the light of the wicked shall be put out, and the spark of his fire shall not shine.

Job 18:5

Bildad tells Job that God is going to finish him off if Job does not agree with them about his iniquity.
Elihu saw the three elders as foolish:

Against his three friends was his wrath kindled, because they had found no answer, and *yet* had condemned Job.

Job 32:3

You see the problem here? It is not that the three men are wrong doctrinally. Their problem was the fact that they assumed things about Job, yet they had no proof! Elihu says, "You have found no answer, and yet you condemn Job. You have no proof, and you condemn him!"

Elihu continues:

> I said, Days should speak, and multitude of years should teach wisdom. But *there is* a spirit in man: and the inspiration of the Almighty giveth them understanding. Great men are not *always* wise: neither do the aged understand judgment. Therefore I said, Hearken to me; I also will show mine opinion. Behold, I waited for your words; I gave ear to your reasons, whilst ye searched out what to say. Yea, I attended unto you, and, behold, *there was* none of you that convinced Job, *or* that answered his words.
>
> Job 32:7-12

In the end, God rebuked Eliphaz, Bildad, and Zophar:

> And it was *so*, that after the LORD had spoken these words unto Job, the LORD said to Eliphaz the Temanite, My wrath is kindled against thee, and against thy two friends: for ye have not spoken of me *the thing that is* right, as my servant Job *hath* . . . . So Eliphaz the Temanite and Bildad the Shuhite *and* Zophar the Naamathite went, and did according as the LORD commanded them: the LORD also accepted Job.
>
> Job 42:7, 9

Elihu was not rebuked. He was considered wise because,

> Now he hath not directed *his* words against me: neither will I answer him with your speeches.
>
> Job 32:14

Elihu was humble. He was content to be silent and to wait for the aged to speak into the situation with Job. You see, Elihu did not just speak because he had knowledge and theology; he refused to be an echo of the other three men. Though he had understanding, he held his peace. He withheld his peace until the unction of the Holy Spirit came upon him.

Dear reader, see the wisdom of Elihu's behavior so we may avoid God's judgments against the proud, as in the case of the three elder men before Job. When the Holy Spirit moved Elihu, he answered:

> I said, I will answer also my part, I also will shew mine opinion. For I am full of matter, the spirit within me constraineth me. Behold, my belly is as wine which hath no vent; it is ready to burst like new bottles. I will speak, that I may be refreshed: I will open my lips and answer. Let me not, I pray you, accept any man's person, neither let me give flattering titles unto man. For I know not to give flattering titles; in so doing my maker would soon take me away.
>
> Job 32:17-22

With great humility he pleads with Job, not out of arrogance, but humility, to hear his words. He comes alongside Job and says that he is a man just like Job. He is not there to think of himself as better or more holy. He understands that it is God who made them both and says that we are both of the clay.

Elihu assures Job that his terror should not make Job afraid, nor his hand be heavy upon him. He is saying that he has not come to crush Job. You can tell his attitude is of the Spirit of God because there is mercy and grace in his speech. But when a man is proud, he gives the appearance of being somewhat other than human.

Most people refuse to do what we say unless there is grace about it:

> He that is of a proud heart stirreth up strife: but he that putteth his trust in the LORD shall be made fat.
>
> Proverbs 28:25

When we claim to be ministering to someone, and we get mad and upset with him because he doesn't follow our advice, that strife comes from the pride in our heart. If the Holy Spirit has been offended, He will deal with him accordingly. But sometimes the individual only leaves knowing he made the minister upset, not God.

> The LORD shall cut off all flattering lips, and the tongue that speaketh proud things: Who have said, with our tongue will we prevail; our lips are our own: who is lord over us? For the oppression of the poor, for the sighing of the needy, now will I arise, saith the LORD; I will set him in safety from him that puffeth at him.
>
> Psalm 12:3-5

From Elihu we learn that, as men, we have no more power than anyone else. It is important to ask in a kind manner. Elihu, by the Spirit of God, manifested by what Paul would later tell the Philippians, we are to consider others as above ourselves.

You may ask friends and family members to do something, but it is their prerogative to say no. If they do, that needs to be okay with you. You may not like their decision, but you are not God. If it is God speaking to them, then God will handle their consequences. If we do not have faith in God to take our words and counsel and use them in their lives, then manipulation is the only alternative.

Someone once said, "An exaggerated sense of your own power can also cause you to feel overly responsible—as if you are indispensable." You think those you counsel will never make it if you do not interfere. This is nothing but pride and arrogance: Without you, the project fails. Without you, the people won't be able to function.

You must learn to do what you can and after that, rest in the fact that there is a God. Accept that you don't have the power to change minds. It is better for you to intercede on their behalf, rather than playing God in their lives. If they don't receive what you say, your rest is in prayer. You give the Word. You speak by the unction of the Holy Ghost. If they don't listen to that, then go before God in prayer and ask Him to work by the Word you spoke to them.

Often, when you interfere, you think you are helping, but all you are doing is enabling them. Sometimes the best thing for a foolish person is to spend the weekend in jail if that is where they brought themselves. Though you don't like it or want it, your intervention can become their damnation. They never have to look to God; they have learned to look to you because your pride has caused you to play God for so long.

I'll take care of you; I'll watch over you. You do what I say, think the way I think, live the way I live, walk the way I walk, and I'll take care of you. If you get into trouble, I will help you.

At this point, you will be playing God in people's lives! If God uses you to help someone, then thank God. But don't pretend as though you did something.

When we involve ourselves in a person's life, it must be in the measure of our authority in his life. Our authority must be exercised with respect and responsibility in his life. When we act beyond our authority in the lives of others, then we are acting in pride. The humble realize that if they have not been given authority by God to involve themselves in someone's life, then they have no responsibility in that life, either. Now, if God gives you authority, then you do have responsibility.

Third, the proud play God by exalting themselves.

He hath said in his heart, God hath forgotten: he hideth his face; he will never see it.

Psalm 10:11

Wherefore let him that thinketh he standeth take heed lest he fall.

1 Corinthians 10:12

Not a novice, lest being lifted up with pride he fall into the condemnation of the devil.

1 Timothy 3:6

In Timothy, we have an individual who appears remarkably spiritual. We would think this individual needs to be put into ministry. Yet Paul says to Timothy, "There are going to be some people who demonstrate a wonderful spiritual life, but be careful. Don't just put a novice into position because from that they could be lifted up with pride and fall into condemnation with the devil."

I have seen wonderful, God-fearing men have this happen to them. Condemnation is judgment. It is possible for one who has a beautiful spiritual life to end up in tragedy, losing God's favor.

I believe this point is relatively simple: Don't think more highly of yourself than you ought. Humble yourself before God and men. Don't let men promote and advance you. Lay your life and all ambitions into the caring hands of God. Refuse pride, refuse promotion, as though it is not something to be grasped. Be content to let God bring into your life all that He desires for you, all that He has prepared and equipped you for! Realize that apart from God, you will not be strong, courageous, or faithful. Never get to a point in your life where you think you could never fall away into some sin or rebellion; forever live trusting in the keeping power of our Lord Jesus Christ!

BREAKING THE STRONGHOLD
OF DEFEAT

CHAPTER 11

Defeat! Consider how effective the stronghold of defeat can be in a believer's life. If the devil can get us to think that we are defeated, then we give up. We don't pray anymore. We don't believe anymore. We don't move forward anymore. We are defeated!

Now, it is imperative that the reader realize that defeat is never a period in a believer's life. God's plans for His children are not for defeat, but victory and a desired end. The Bible says that He has given to us the victory through our Lord Jesus Christ; we are more than conquerors; we are overcomers in this life! Therefore, we must not settle for what appears to be defeat.

In my life, there have been times when I settled for defeat because I listened to the lies of my enemy. I actually found myself agreeing to the absurdities he was feeding me: "It's all over now! They will never be saved now. They will never listen to you now. Nothing will ever change."

However, faith never comes to defeat! Faith always rises up with the answer of God. Faith always overcomes; it always prevails; it always believes! If we as believers do not break the stronghold of defeat, Satan can cause us to give up and embrace unbelief. We must not allow the devil to bring us to a place of defeat.

Defeat is a spirit that gives up.

It puts stones over Lazarus' tomb.

It sends crowds home because they cannot see any means of being fed.

It sells birthrights for a bowl of soup.

The Bible mentions defeat by exposing the faithlessness of those who had fainted when instead God had wanted them to prevail. Fainting and defeat are often the same thing. Someone was defeated when God sought for a man and could find none! Somewhere that man was defeated. Every time we tell God, "No!" because of fear or feelings of inadequacy, saying, "Woe is me . . . . How could You ever do anything with my life?" then we are suffering from defeat. Every time we excuse ourselves from serving God because of past sins, then we are succumbing to defeat rather than taking the victory that is ours through the blood of Jesus Christ.

Before we examine the means by which we may overcome defeat, first let the reader consider the reality and cause of believers being defeated.

We Are Tempted to Faint When We Conclude That Prayer Is Not Working

> Men ought always to pray, and not to faint; Saying, There was in a city a judge, which feared not God, neither regarded man: And there was a widow in that city; and she came unto him, saying, Avenge me of mine adversary. And he would not for a while: but afterward he said within himself, Though I fear not God, nor regard man; Yet because this widow troubleth me, I will avenge her, lest by her continual coming she weary me. And the Lord said, Hear what the unjust judge saith. And shall not God avenge his own elect, which cry day and night unto him, though he bear long with them? I tell you that he will avenge them speedily. Nevertheless when the Son of man cometh, shall he find faith on the earth?
>
> Luke 18:1-8

Jesus' analogy is that if an unjust judge can be moved by a persistent widow, then how much more will a just God be moved by the prayers of His saints. You see, it is in prayer that the devil wants to defeat us. When we go to prayer and an immediate answer is not realized, when it seems like all is lost and it is too late, it is then that Satan tempts us to faint in prayer. Consider the example of Mary and

Martha. They prayed to Jesus to come heal Lazarus. An immediate answer was not realized; it appeared all was lost, and Jesus showed up too late—Lazarus had been dead and buried for four days. In mourning and heartbreak, they accused Jesus of not helping. They thought He failed them because He did not answer their prayer the way they wanted Him to answer it.

For some, this is exactly where you are today. You have given up on prayer. You have sealed the tomb of your dead dreams. You have settled on some defeated notion that God has failed. You ask, therefore, "Why pray? Why trouble God anymore? It is over for me!"

Or maybe you have given up on a spouse being saved or a child being healed. Perhaps you have given up on our nation, and you no longer pray for revival; therefore, it is given over to paganism and the ungodly. And perhaps your heart is saying, "What is the use of prayer? God has not raised anyone to lead our nation in the paths of righteousness. There are no prophets in the pulpits anymore."

Just as Mary and Martha were discouraged, their defeat was not permanent because they could still trust God. Though things had not gone the way they wanted, their defeat was turned into victory when they rolled the stone from Lazarus' grave! Likewise, we must not be defeated in the area of prayer! I know things come into our lives that break our hearts. Sometimes it comes out of nowhere, and sometimes we see it coming. When our hearts have been broken through devastating circumstances like the loss of a child or the betrayal of a spouse, it makes us want to give up. Our hearts begin to say, "What is the use? Why try anymore? What is the use in trying to be a friend? They are all going to stab me in the back anyway." Oh, believer, we must pray; we must believe there is a God who moves mountains. We can never let Satan have the last word. We must always answer that adversary upon the sure promises of God. Do not let him tell you what will be. By God, you tell him what is! Don't let Satan have the last word; tell him, "The Lord is faithful to all his promises and loving toward all he has made" (Psalm 145:13).

Sometimes, in prayer, the only way we are not going to faint is by leaning upon the promises of God's Word. Often we go before God when there is much hope, when we can see a very real solution to the problem. But sometimes God waits until we can no longer see a solution; it appears that all is lost. But if you can still believe in a God who answers prayer, if you refuse to faint and will be determined to touch this God, you will find that He can move those mountains and roll back those gravestones and resurrect your dead dreams and hopes.

To fail in prayer is to fail in every area of life. If we have given up on prayer, then we have given up on God. If we have given up on God, then it is over! God has not abandoned you. "Can a mother forget the baby at her breast and have no compassion on the child she has borne? Though she may forget, I will not forget you" (Isaiah 49:15). Oh, God, You do not forget me! You hear me praying! Though I may see no evidence of the fact, I can rest upon Your sure promises that You are my salvation and hope! "Never will I leave you; never will I forsake you" (Hebrews 13:5). "Since ancient times no one has heard, no ear has perceived, no eye has seen any God besides you, who acts on behalf of those who wait for him" (Isaiah 64:4). Oh, how I have leaned hard upon these promises. I have waited for God, and He has never failed me! People have even asked why I continue to wait upon God when it appeared the situation was over. But I could not let go of Him who promised! "My soul, wait silently for God alone, for my expectation is from Him" (Psalm 62:5).

When my enemies surround me, my expectation is of God. I know that He has a company of angels watching over me, but my expectancy is that the warrior of heaven will suddenly come upon my enemies.

When I am sick, I am not expecting my healing to come through somebody's hand; I am expecting my Healer to touch my life! I am expecting my God to come, my God to answer, my God to minister to my needs.

We Are Tempted to Faint When Our Good Works Fail to Produce Fruit

And let us not be weary in well doing: for in due season we shall reap, if we faint not. As we have therefore opportunity, let us do good unto all *men*, especially unto them who are of the household of faith.

Galatians 6:9-10

The Lord has been true to this promise for all my life. I remember when we started the church. I prayed for the Lord to give me faithful men—men that I can count on, men who will pray, men who will minister, men who will preach, men who will lead.

There were men that God gave me who are still with me to this day, and I am very thankful for them. But it took ten years for that fruit to be seen! Then, after ten years, the Lord began to give me fruit. The promise was being fulfilled. God was raising up men of prayer, men who would preach, men who would go to Russia, to the prisons, and to the streets.

There were times I wanted to faint and give up. I would say, "All I ever do is give. I give money to those who need money. I give kind words, but seldom is there a kind word in return." And the Holy Ghost would say to me, "Don't quit. Don't faint. One day you will be smothered with kind words. You just look for every opportunity to sow."

If we are not careful, it is possible to give up and be defeated in the area of good works. Remember that we never see the fruit as fast as we want to see it. But just as sure as the seed is sown, it will bring forth its righteous fruit if we don't faint.

We Are Tempted to Faint When We Are Hated and Outnumbered by Our Enemies

Wherefore seeing we also are compassed about with so great a cloud of witnesses, let us lay aside every weight, and the sin which doth so easily beset *us*, and let us run with patience the race that is set before us, Looking unto Jesus the author and finisher of *our* faith; who for the joy that was set before him endured the cross, despising the shame, and is set down at the right hand of the throne of God. For consider him that endured such contradiction of sinners against himself, lest ye be wearied and faint in your minds. Ye have not yet resisted unto blood, striving against sin.

Hebrews 12:1-4

If you are going to live for Christ, then you will be hated by those who hate Him. If they called Him a devil, they will call you one. They will not appreciate your message of righteousness. They will not appreciate your gospel because there is no room for man to parade his own glory before God. A lot of times you may feel as though you are the only one left. It is at that point you want to give up.

Elijah also thought he was the only one faithful to God. He wanted to give up and die! Many times Moses wanted to give up, but he continued to press on. The Bible says that Moses endured because he saw Him who is invisible. The apostle Paul, when everyone forsook him, said that the Lord stood with him. When it seemed like they were all by themselves, Moses and Paul endured because God manifested His presence to them in a very special way.

When you are suffering, and feeling outnumbered when those who are Christians never speak up and speak out, when it seems like you are the only one standing for the Lord, and as a result, you are getting all the reproach and hardship, it is very tempting to quit and give up. As did Elijah, you begin to think, "What difference can I make when there are tens of thousands that stand against me and it appears that no one stands with me?" If you look at how many are against you, then it is possible to faint in your mind. But remember that you and God are always a majority. With God, there are always more for you than there are those who are against you.

We Are Tempted to Faint When We Are Persecuted

But call to remembrance the former days, in which, after ye were illuminated, ye endured a great fight of afflictions; Partly, whilst ye were made a gazingstock both by reproaches and afflictions; and partly, whilst ye became companions of them that were so used. For ye had compassion of me in my bonds, and took joyfully the spoiling of your goods, knowing in yourselves that ye have in heaven a better and an enduring substance. Cast not away therefore your confidence, which hath great recompense of reward. Now the just shall live by faith: but if *any man* draw back, my soul shall have no pleasure in him. But we are not of them who draw back unto perdition; but of them that believe to the saving of the soul.

Hebrews 10:32-35, 38-39

There can be a confidence in our lives that we are not going to be defeated. We will move on.

Solomon said, "If thou faint in the day of adversity, thy strength is small" (Proverbs 24:10).

When I used to see people fainting in adversity, I thought they were so weak. I would say to myself, "If that were me, I would never act the way they act." I considered myself to be so strong. But as I pondered Solomon's wisdom, I realized that he is simply describing the strength of man—all men, even me. He was describing me! He is telling me how small man is and that he will always faint in adversity. But those who belong to God have a greater strength and hope because of this promise:

Hast thou not known? Hast thou not heard, that the everlasting God, the Lord, the Creator of the ends of the earth, fainteth not, neither is weary? There is no searching of his understanding. He giveth power to the faint; and to them that have no might he increaseth strength. Even the youths shall faint and be weary, and the young men shall utterly fall: But they that wait upon the Lord shall renew their strength; they shall mount up with wings as eagles; they shall run, and not be weary; and they shall walk, and not faint.

Isaiah 40:28-31

That is how you transform your small strength for His omnipotent power. When you wait upon God, refusing to give up in the face of persecution, affliction, and trials, it confounds the enemy! For all practical purposes, you should be defeated by now, but you are waiting upon the Lord. People may marvel and say, "How are you ever going to overcome this?" And the overcomer in you says, "I don't know, but when I do, I will be saying that the Lord is my helper!" You will be able to declare as Micah, "Don't rejoice over me, my enemies, for when I am down, the Lord will be a light to me, and He will pick me up!"

You will be able to say as Habakkuk, "Though the fig tree does not blossom, and there be no figs upon the vine; though the flock shall all be scattered, and there be no cattle in the stalls; though the olive tree shall cast its fruit, and there be no grain to grind, I will yet trust in the Lord. He will make my feet like hinds' feet. I will rest upon mine high places." You are not going to be defeated or overcome.

We Are Tempted to Faint and Forsake the Body When It Seems Jesus Is Not Coming Soon

> And let us consider one another to provoke unto love and to good works: Not forsaking the assembling of ourselves together, as the manner of some *is*; but exhorting *one another*: and so much the more, as ye see the day approaching.
> Hebrews 10:24-25

The temptation of the last days is to forsake the assembly. The distraction of other things will attempt to dominate our time. The long-awaited coming of Christ will appear to be nothing more than a far-fetched dream. The Bible says that believers will become negligent of His body, being drawn to temporal and empty things. Even today, many are asking, "Where is the promise of Jesus' coming? Why hasn't He come yet?"

This attitude will cause many to forsake the unique relationship that the body of Christ is to share: a relationship where fellow believers can provoke one another to good works, stir one another up to love, and encourage one another to be involved in the proper activities of building God's kingdom prior to the coming of Jesus Christ.

If you believe that Jesus is coming soon, you will be among those who are expecting Him as well. But many faint in this area because they think that His coming is far away.

Though many believers have fainted in the above areas, thank God they didn't live there! They arose! You see, if you have fainted and your spiritual life is coming to a sudden stop, and you are practically wasting away in defeat, there is still hope for you. As a believer, this is not your end. You do not have to settle for this lame condition. There is power in God, power in the risen Christ to raise you up. If you are in Christ, you are an overcomer. You can get up. You can go on in Jesus' name! Nothing is more pitiful than defeated Christians; they are so negative, so pessimistic, so downcast. The devil would love to parade you around as his defeated trophy. Refuse him that glory, and let Jesus prevail for you. Here is how you can overcome. I would like to show you three things God has given in His Word to break the stronghold of defeat.

Breaking the Stronghold of Defeat
First, you must believe in the end that God has for your life.

> Who shall separate us from the love of Christ? *shall* tribulation, or distress, or persecution, or famine, or nakedness, or peril, or sword? As it is written, For thy sake we are killed all the day long; we are accounted as sheep for the slaughter. Nay, in all these things we are more than conquerors through him that loved us. For I am persuaded, that neither death, nor life, nor angels, nor principalities, nor powers, nor things present, nor things to come, Nor height, nor depth, nor any other creature, shall be able to separate us from the love of God, which is in Christ Jesus our Lord.
>
> Romans 8:35-39

Though many things may be at work, nothing can separate you from God! To have seen the apostle Paul in prison, you never would have thought he was the prisoner. He was the one singing and rejoicing. He was more than a conqueror.

As a believer, you are inseparable from Jesus Christ. Nothing can come between you and the Lord. You are more than a conqueror! If your life is to overcome defeat, then refuse to settle for what is. Keep your eyes on what will be. Never allow present affliction to rob you of future glory. Never allow the devil and his lies to cause you to believe this is all there is to life.

Because you cannot be separated from Jesus, this means that nothing can keep you from Jesus. Jesus is your refuge. For example, He is your refuge from your own emotions. As disturbed as the emotions can get, they cannot separate you from Jesus. Your mood cannot keep you from Jesus. Even your sins cannot keep you from Jesus. Weakness will not keep you from Him; it will actually draw Him to you. When everybody has forsaken, He is your constant companion. Even your needs do not prevent His presence; He meets everyone by His great wealth. Never fix your gaze on the mountain, the adversity, or the enemies. Look away to Jesus and what He will make of it all. Nothing can keep Jesus from you. He will be faithful to the very end. He will never forsake you. To overcome defeat, you must be convinced that nothing in the end will defeat your life in Christ!

Second, you must receive the victory in defeat. If you are going to break the stronghold of defeat, then in the defeat, you must receive the victory. It was in the fire that the three Hebrews received the victory. It was in the lions' den that Daniel received the victory. It was in the contest with Goliath that David received the victory.

I will assure you that without God, we will face many things in life that will defeat us. Life will crush us!

Mary and Martha were in a situation that naturally spelled defeat; Lazarus was dead. But in the tragedy, they received the victory and rolled the stone away; Lazarus was raised up.

In the moments that spell defeat, you must reach up into heaven and take the victory! "And he said unto me, Son of man, can these bones live? And I answered, O Lord GOD, thou knowest" (Ezekiel 37:3).

A defeated person would never preach a sermon to a dead corpse like those scattered throughout the valley. They were dead and dry bones; they had no ears to hear. But God said to prophesy, and in the appearance of defeat, Ezekiel began to prophesy, and the victory came.

The overcomer, when he is faced with defeat, acts out of victory. When the grandchildren have crossed the line, perhaps they have turned to the occult, and it seems they have totally given themselves over to rebellion, you or somebody had better be able to reach up into heaven and touch God for the victory! Somebody in that place of defeat must start prophesying. The Word of God must go forth, and those wayward children will come back to Christ!

You cannot settle for defeat because God has made you more than a conqueror. The doctor gave you the report. You have cancer and three months to live. Well, that is what the doctor said, and it sure spells defeat. But what is God saying? Can God remove that cancer from the body? You are not dead yet; therefore, it is not over. There is a victory to be had. Somebody has to have the faith to speak to the cancer and tell it to go away. If you cannot receive victory, you will receive defeat!

What kind of God is He, and what kind of people are we, if He can only sustain His people on the mountain? God's desire is to bring us right into the valley of peril and death. It is there that He will dismay and frustrate the enemy! God will show that in the darkest moments of our lives and the trials of our faith, He still has a people who are rejoicing in the victory.

Even Jesus wrestled it. Fiery darts were filling the spiritual night. The tranquility of His soul was broken: "Now is my soul troubled" (John 12:27).

Jesus taught us in Gethsemane how to fight back by believing God. In His darkest hour, notice what Jesus did to combat the enemy:

- He chose close friends to be with Him. This is very similar to the exhortation in Hebrews not to forsake the assembly, but to encourage and provoke one another to love and good works.
- According to Matthew, He opened His soul to them (Matthew 26:38).
- He asked for their intercession and partnership (Matthew 26:39).
- His hope was not in friends, but in His heavenly Father (Matthew 26:39).
- He rested in the wisdom of His Father.
- He fixed His eyes on the future, rather than the present cup He had to drink.

Like Elijah, many tend to push the friends away when on the verge of fainting. Even now, people push the church away and the comfort and wisdom they could find in the body of Christ.

Listen, when you are suffering and going through a trial, it is not the time to forsake the body of Christ—the people who know and love you. Don't be defeated when people let you down. The disciples fell asleep on Jesus, but He didn't cast off their friendship, and neither should you. Let your firm hope be in your heavenly Father, not your friends, though you seek their intercession and companionship.

Third, you must understand why you are brought to the edge of defeat.

Paul told us in 2 Corinthians 4:1, 16 that he was able to keep from fainting by receiving mercy from God.

Look at Paul in brokenness, weakness, and feebleness. He is in death often, despairing for life, in prison, beat times without number, five times whipped by the Jews, three times beaten with rods, once stoned, three times shipwrecked.

If all this were not enough, he spent a night and a day in the ocean. He took frequent journeys. He was in constant danger—dangers from rivers, dangers from robbers, dangers from his own people, dangers from the Gentiles, dangers in the city, dangers in the wilderness, dangers in the sea, and dangers among false brethren! He was in labors often. Even Paul described it as hardships—sleepless nights, hunger and thirst, often without food, and exposed to the cold!

Oh, Paul, "How did you do it?" Paul might have said, "I received His mercy so that I wouldn't faint."

> We which live are always delivered unto death for Jesus' sake, that the life also of Jesus might be made manifest in our mortal flesh. For which cause we faint not; but though our outward man perish, yet the inward *man* is renewed day by day.
>
> 2 Corinthians 4:11, 16

Just as God delivered Jesus over to death by the determined counsel of God (Acts 2:23-24), so God hands over His servants.

Why? Because it is not possible that you should be holden of death any more than Jesus would be, seeing it is His life within your clay!

If you are always putting yourself in comfortable places and God never allows any adversity to come, then the life of Jesus will rarely be manifested.

The more of Christ that is in you, the more afflictions you can face; the more persecution you can endure. In the end, this will work for you wonderful weights of reward in heaven. So Paul says that is what he looked upon. He counted on the eternal weight of glory.

What God is allowing you to face is not to destroy you. His purpose is that His Son may demonstrate His power in you by overcoming. You could never be a demonstration of His life and overcome hell if you faint when adversity strikes!

So why are you not defeated? Because God is not defeated! Why are you not worried? Because God is not worried! He loves you too much to let you give up and be afraid.

You see, the simple way of receiving victory is to have faith. Faith is to hear God in the moment of the trial. What would have become of Lazarus if Mary and Martha had not heard Jesus tell them to remove the stone from his tomb?

Overcoming defeat is:

Martha demanding the stone be removed. Peter forsaking the boats after his sin. Paul preaching after the stoning. And you, _____, getting up after being _____ and going on to being useful.

> Listen,
>> We may die for this...
>>> We will suffer for this...
>>>> We will not be rewarded in or by the world...

> But in the end:
>> We will have our faith,
>>> We will have run the race,
>>>> We will have fought a good fight,
>>>>> We will have WON!

NOTES

Chapter 2
1. Jan Silvious, Look at It This Way (Colorado Springs, Colorado: WATERBROOK PRESS, 2003), 24-25.
2. Jan Silvious, Look at It This Way (Colorado Springs, Colorado: WATERBROOK PRESS, 2003), 32.

Chapter 3
1. Jan Silvious, Look at It This Way (Colorado Springs, Colorado: WATERBROOK PRESS, 2003), 38-39.
2. Jan Silvious, Look at It This Way (Colorado Springs, Colorado: WATERBROOK PRESS, 2003), 48.
3. Jan Silvious, Look at It This Way (Colorado Springs, Colorado: WATERBROOK PRESS, 2003), 27-28.

Chapter 4
1. Devern Fromke, Life's Ultimate Privilege (Cloverdale, Indiana: Sure Foundation, 1986) Day Ten 3-4.
2. Jan Silvious, Look at It This Way (Colorado Springs, Colorado: WATERBROOK PRESS, 2003), 38-39.
3. Devern Fromke, Life's Ultimate Privilege (Cloverdale, Indiana: Sure Foundation, 1986) Day Ten 2-3.

Chapter 9

1. Barbara Johnson, Pack Up Your Gloomees in a Great Big Box, then sit on the lid and laugh! (Word Publishing, 1993), 118-119.

2. Barbara Johnson, Pain Is Inevitable, but Misery Is Optional. (Word Publishing, 1990), 16, 82.

ABOUT THE AUTHOR

Pastor Lee Shipp, as the founder and senior pastor of First New Testament Church, has ministered God's Word through the power of the Holy Spirit for more than twenty years. Led by a devotion to his Savior and a love for the Scripture, he has been used by God to teach and preach throughout the world, through conferences, camp meetings, and revivals. Pastor Shipp is also founder and president of A Call to the Heart, a ministry of evangelism and outreach through radio, TV, literature, and national and international campaigns. Pastor Shipp and his family live in Baton Rouge, Louisiana, where they continue to serve the Lord with their church family.

CONTACT PAGE

To contact Pastor Shipp for ministry, he may be reached at:

First New Testament Church
3235 Aubin Lane
Baton Rouge, LA 70816
USA

(225) 293-2222

Pastor Shipp's email address is:
Office@fntchurch.org
ctoh@fntchurch.org
gospelshipp@hotmail.com

Please visit us at: www.fntchurch.org.

CPSIA information can be obtained at www.ICGtesting.com
Printed in the USA
LVOW06s1038080814

398075LV00003B/3/A